# Enterprise Business Intelligence and Data Warehousing

# Enterprise Business Intelligence and Data Warehousing
## Program Management Essentials

Alan Simon

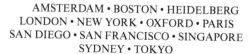

AMSTERDAM • BOSTON • HEIDELBERG
LONDON • NEW YORK • OXFORD • PARIS
SAN DIEGO • SAN FRANCISCO • SINGAPORE
SYDNEY • TOKYO

Morgan Kaufmann is an imprint of Elsevier

Morgan Kaufmann is an imprint of Elsevier
225 Wyman Street, Waltham, MA 02451, USA

**Notices**
Knowledge and best practice in this field are constantly changing. As new research and experience broaden our understanding, changes in research methods, professional practices, or medical treatment may become necessary.

Practitioners and researchers must always rely on their own experience and knowledge in evaluating and using any information, methods, compounds, or experiments described herein. In using such information or methods they should be mindful of their own safety and the safety of others, including parties for whom they have a professional responsibility.

To the fullest extent of the law, neither the Publisher nor the authors, contributors, or editors, assume any liability for any injury and/or damage to persons or property as a matter of products liability, negligence or otherwise, or from any use or operation of any methods, products, instructions, or ideas contained in the material herein.

**British Library Cataloguing-in-Publication Data**
A catalogue record for this book is available from the British Library.

**Library of Congress Cataloging-in-Publication Data**
A catalog record for this book is available from the Library of Congress.

ISBN: 978-0-12-801540-7

For Information on all Morgan Kaufmann publications
visit our website at http://store.elsevier.com/

Working together
to grow libraries in
developing countries

www.elsevier.com • www.bookaid.org

# CONTENTS

# ABOUT THE AUTHOR

Alan Simon is a Senior Lecturer in the Information Systems Department at Arizona State University's WP Carey School of Business. He is also the Managing Principal of Thinking Helmet, Inc., a boutique consultancy specializing in enterprise business intelligence and data management architecture.

Alan has authored or coauthored 30 technology and business books dating back to 1985. He has previously led national or global BI and data warehousing practices at several consultancies, and has provided enterprise data management architecture and roadmap services to more than 40 clients dating back to the early 1990s. From 1987 to 1992 Alan was a software developer and product manager with Digital Equipment Corporation's Database Systems Group, and earlier he was a United States Air Force Computer Systems Officer stationed at Cheyenne Mountain, Colorado.

Alan received his bachelor's degree from Arizona State University and his master's degree from the University of Arizona, and is a native of Pittsburgh.

## INTRODUCTION: A PROVOCATIVE QUESTION

*Are business intelligence and data warehousing dying disciplines?*

The above question might seem an odd one given that this book covers best practices for managing and leading an enterprise-scale business intelligence (BI) and data warehousing (DW) program, but it's one that needs to be asked. At the time of this book's publication (2015) a simple Internet search will turn up numerous articles, white papers, and blogs proclaiming – and perhaps even celebrating – the impending death of the BI/DW era that began in the 1989–1991 time frame. "A quarter century of so many under-delivering or even failed BI/DW efforts is enough!" the mantra goes, and then continues: "the age of Big Data and analytics has arrived to save us!"

I would contend that the answer to this question isn't quite the "slam dunk yes!" that many analysts, consultants, and other observers would argue. Certainly, we've seen more than our share of enterprise data warehousing (EDW) and enterprise business intelligence (EBI) program shortfalls and outright failures over the past quarter century, for reasons that we'll explore in Chapter 1. However, to claim that the BI/DW era is now concluded and has been – or will soon be – supplanted by the realm of Big Data/analytics isn't entirely accurate, at least in my opinion.

The underpinnings of the "data warehousing versus Big Data" and "business intelligence versus analytics" twin debates are, in fact, very much driven by terminology and how one actually defines these various disciplines and what their various scopes include *and don't include*. Many who argue that BI and DW are on their way out base their contentions on defining BI as either of the following:

- Solely a view into the past – that is, data-driven insights that fit the paradigm of "tell me what happened and why"
- The above-mentioned "tell me what happened and why" data-driven insights along with "tell me what is happening right now" – that is, real-time insights, also drawn directly from an organization's data assets

In this view, however, future-looking, hypothesis-formulating insights of the "tell me what is likely to happen and why" variety are typically *not* considered to be part of the BI realm. BI is one thing, while analytics are another; at least that's what some would contend.

They will also point out that the underlying data warehouses typically housed in relational database management systems (DBMSs) built to support this classic BI functionality aren't well suited to provide future-looking predictive analytics. Therefore, the argument goes, a dichotomy between classic BI and DW versus this emerging era of predictive analytics – along with the Big Data engines that support analytical functionality – must exist. And so we must be dealing with *two* competing sets of sibling disciplines: BI/DW *versus* Big Data/analytics.

With regards to the above, many analysts and consultants do correctly point out that classic BI that looks at the past and perhaps also the present is increasingly *not* sufficient for the broad range of insights needed in today's fast-paced business world. Analytics are the wave of the future to identify and interdict potential problems before they actually occur or at least before those problems get too bad, the argument goes. And on the flip side, analytics are also a means to identify high-impact potential business *opportunities* much earlier than with hindsight-focused, classic BI.

In fact, by adding discovery-oriented analytics to the mix – that is, "tell me something interesting and important from mining through mountains of data" – modern Big Data-driven analytics might identify business opportunities and potential problems that classic BI might never discover and deliver at all. Given this new generation of data-driven insights, who could argue with the merits of analytics?

By my way of thinking, though, the argument shouldn't be "business intelligence versus analytics" or "data warehousing versus Big Data" with one or the other being the "winner" for the next quarter century or so. To the contrary, the contention that is the foundation of this book is that BI should be thought of as a continuum that *also includes* forward-looking *and* discovery-oriented analytics, and, likewise, DW is a sort of "über-discipline" that is certainly evolving to an era of nonrelational technology (i.e., Big Data) – *but still must support the <u>entire</u> continuum of BI functionality*.

In a companion book to this text entitled *Modern Enterprise Business Intelligence and Data Management: A Roadmap for IT Directors, Managers, and Architects* (Simon, 2014) I refer back to my own writings from close to 20 years ago (Simon, 1997) as well as my class lecture notes from Arizona State University (Simon, 2013–2014) in which I proposed that BI is best defined as a continuum containing *all* of the following capabilities:

- Tell what happened, and why
- Tell what is happening right now, and why
- Tell what is likely to happen, and why
- Tell what might have happened if we had done something different, and why
- Tell something interesting and important without me asking a specific question

By my way of thinking, BI has – or at least should have – *always* included a view into the past, the present, the future, and the "hidden" (via discovery-oriented, "tell me something interesting and important ..." analytics). I will certainly concede that most BI implementations, whether enterprise-scale or departmental-level, have ended up focusing primarily or solely on hindsight-facing "tell me what happened and why" insights. In fact, I would go a step further: far too many BI implementations over the past quarter century have actually produced very little other than static or lightly parameterized reports that often provide very little in the way of actionable insights.

Likewise, many DW implementations over the years have been difficult endeavors for reasons related to their underlying relational database technology and/or the multidimensional cubes used for "slice and dice" BI capabilities. In the early days of the BI/DW era, database capacity and performance were significant issues. Even as the underlying database engines dramatically improved in core technology, capacity, and usability, they still weren't particularly well suited toward the types of model-driven analytics that have come to form the foundation of today's world of *data science*. For most organizations, the predecessors to today's "data science" were accomplished by statisticians and mathematical modelers who usually did their own data acquisition, management, and analysis in a manner totally disjoint from any formal DW implementations.

Certainly, Big Data technology has rocked the world of data-driven insights, especially when it comes to predictive and discovery-oriented analytics. But the point I would argue is that Big Data and its accompanying analytics do not supplant classic BI and DW; *instead they do a fantastic job filling in the missing pieces on that portion of the BI continuum that <u>should</u> have been in place all along!*

Is there still a role for classic online analytical processing (OLAP) BI functionality that provides critical insights into "tell me what happened and why?" I would argue: absolutely! Are real-time BI dashboards that provide critical "tell me what is happening right now" insights still valuable? Again, in my opinion: absolutely!

Now the big question: are classic OLAP and real-time insights enhanced by the emerging realm of Big Data technology? Once again: absolutely!

This opinion of a continuum of capabilities encompassing classic BI and DW along with emerging Big Data and analytics isn't solely mine. For example, Dr. Ralph Kimball, a well-known and widely followed BI/DW thought leader for many years, offers the proposition of the "Hadoop data warehouse" (Brandwein, 2014). Similarly, Jeff Kelly of The Wikibon Project and Bill Schmarzo, the Chief Technology Officer for Enterprise Information Management (EIM) at EMC, advocate the idea that you should "Hadoop-ify your data warehouse" (Kelly and Schmarzo, 2014).

Additionally, IBM recently released a *Big Data & Analytics for a Smarter Enterprise* infographic (IBM, 2014) that depicts:

- An integrated collection of data repositories housing operational data; a landing area, exploration area, and active archive zone for data; another data zone for deep analytics; and also an *EDW and data mart zone*
- Data from the above-mentioned zones feeding into an integrated set of capabilities that tell users *all* of the following:
  - "What is happening?" (discovery and exploration)
  - "Why did it happen?" (reporting and analysis)
  - "What did I learn?" and "What's best?" (cognitive)
  - "What action should I take?" (decision management)
  - "What could happen?" (predictive analytics and modeling)

As represented in the view expressed by IBM's infographic, they appear to embrace the concept of a BI–analytics continuum in terms of capabilities and usage paradigms that transcends labels and terminology.

## THIS BOOK'S PREMISES

Based on the above narrative, we now get to the fundamental premises that underlie the subject matter of this book, which are:

1. BI and DW are *not* dying (or already dead) disciplines, but they *are* and *should be* executed differently today and tomorrow (i.e., 2015 and onwards) than they were a quarter century ago – or for that matter, even 4 or 5 years ago before Big Data technology burst onto the scene.
2. Definitions for "BI" abound, and anyone is free to include whatever types of data-driven insights one feels like including in any given definition. For purposes of this book, though, BI capabilities will include the full continuum discussed earlier: past, present, future, and hidden/unknown. Essentially, BI should be thought of as an "umbrella" for the entire spectrum of data-driven insights, ranging from reports to OLAP to dashboards to predictive analytics to discovery-oriented analytics to guided analytical applications.
3. Similarly, as organizations increasingly build their DW environments (at least in part) on top of Hadoop-based technology, one can feel confident in declaring the following: "Data warehousing *as a discipline* isn't going anywhere; rather, we're bringing in a new generation of technology that will help us realize many of the unrealized promises of data warehouse projects of the past. Relational technology will share the spotlight with Big Data for now and may indeed be supplanted by Big Data in the not-too-distant future; but the 'spirit' of data warehousing – i.e., synthesizing content from many different sources with synergistic results and for relatively easy consumption and usage – will remain for a long time."
4. And now we get to the primary reason for this particular book: BI and DW are certainly challenging disciplines, and, as just noted, evolving right before our eyes. However, *enterprise-scale* BI and DW – regardless of definitions and underlying technology – is *and will continue to be* a daunting proposition.

In the early days of DW, one commonly saw high-level architecture diagrams that depicted dozens upon dozens of source systems feeding data into a single, centralized, and monolithic EDW. However, as we all found out soon enough, those elegant, neatly lined up high-level architecture diagrams were exceedingly difficult – if not outright impossible – to actually implement in full. And many EDWs that actually were implemented and went operational were often unsustainable for more than a couple of years due to the technology limitations with which we had to cope 20–25 years ago.

Even as BI tools, DBMSs, and supporting technologies such as master data management (MDM) engines and extraction, transformation, and loading (ETL) tools evolved and improved over the years, enterprise-scale BI and DW proved as elusive as ever for reasons we will explore in Chapter 1. Until recently, many organizations had simply given up on the idea of building EDWs to deliver EBI; instead they focused their data-driven insights efforts on building collections of departmental data marts that *hopefully* complied with best practices such as conformed dimensions to support at least rudimentary "apples to apples" reports and insights.

But here we are, at the dawn of the Big Data era that – again – in the opinion of this author, and in the spirit of this book, is best thought of as the next wave of BI/DW rather than its successor. Even better: the Big Data era brings new life and new hope to the pursuit of enterprise-scale BI/DW.

Still, we need more than just a new generation of technology to make EBI/EDW a reality. We need program managers and leaders who can learn from the successes and failures of the past and apply those lessons to today's and tomorrow's initiatives in the pursuit of enterprise-level, data-driven insights.

And that's what you'll find in the pages that follow.

## REFERENCES

Brandwein, M., 2014. Building a Hadoop data warehouse: Hadoop 101 for enterprise data professionals – Dr. Ralph Kimball answers your questions. Cloudera. Available from: <http://vision.cloudera.com/building-a-hadoop-data-warehouse-hadoop-101-for-enterprise-data-professionals-dr-ralph-kimball-answers-your-questions/>.

IBM, 2014. Big Data & Analytics for a Smarter Enterprise. IBM Corporation.

Kelly, J., Schmarzo, B., 2014. Create your Big Data vision and Hadoop-ify your data warehouse. Available from: <http://www.slideshare.net/emcacademics/create-your-big-data-vision-and-hadoopify-your-data-warehouse>.

Simon, A., 1997. Better tools, better decisions. *Byte*. January.

Simon, A., 2013–2014. Class Lecture Materials, CIS 394/405: Business Intelligence. Arizona State University, Tempe, AZ.

Simon, A., 2014. Modern Enterprise Business Intelligence and Data Management: A Roadmap for IT Directors, Managers, and Architects. Morgan Kaufmann Publishers, Waltham, MA.

## CHAPTER 1

# The Challenge of Managing and Leading the Enterprise BI/DW Program

## CHAPTER INTRODUCTION

We began the book's Preface with a question, and we will do the same in this first chapter. Our question to now ponder is as follows:

*Why, since the dawn of the business intelligence and data warehousing era, has enterprise business intelligence and data warehousing been so incredibly difficult to achieve?*

Certainly, we can find instances of successful *true* enterprise-scale BI/DW efforts (i.e., an EDW that actually contains and manages the critical mass of data used for a company's or governmental agency's business intelligence needs, rather than a smaller-scale data warehouse or data mart with the word "enterprise" simply tacked onto its description). These enterprise-scale success stories aren't nearly as common as we would hope, though, given that at the time of this writing (late 2014) a quarter century has passed since BI and data warehousing came upon the scene as the 1980s gave way to the 1990s. Still, if one were to survey a healthy sample of data warehouses, data marts, operational data stores (ODSs), and other "reporting databases" that have been built at some time during the past quarter century, the overwhelming majority of them will be found to serve departmental-level needs, or the reports and BI needed for only a handful of an organization's business processes.

In this chapter we will explore why enterprise-scale BI and data warehousing has been so difficult to achieve, as well as – the good news, finally – why the tide seems to be turning in recent years with an increasing number of enterprise-level success stories.

Why the history lesson? Because any enterprise business intelligence and data warehousing (EBI/EDW) program manager or program management team needs to understand the inertia that today's initiatives need to overcome. The "threats" are still out there, and ignorance of the many challenges EBI/EDW efforts have historically faced *and still face* puts a program manager at a distinct disadvantage. Quoting philosopher and author George Santayana (1863–1952), "Those who cannot remember the past, are condemned to repeat it." Since so many of today's enterprise BI/DW program managers haven't experienced the full 25 years' worth of the modern era of business intelligence and data warehousing – and indeed may be relative newcomers to the information technology profession – this chapter helps them "remember" that which they may not have actually experienced.

And for those readers who are indeed long-time BI/DW practitioners, the consolidated collection of EBI/EDW challenges presented in this chapter, along with the discussion of what is changing to help counteract those challenges, will provide that "one-stop shopping" of important information that hallmarks what we try to achieve in the BI/DW world for our end users.

## THE CHALLENGES OF ENTERPRISE-SCALE BI AND DATA WAREHOUSING

Among the many significant challenges over the years to successfully building data warehouses and BI capabilities at the enterprise scale we find:

- Immature technology, at least in the early days of the modern BI/DW era
- The backlash from early EDW failures
- Companies and governmental agencies also focusing on many other competing high-profile enterprise initiatives
- "The need for speed"
- The devaluation of enterprise-level BI versus "subenterprise" reporting and insights
- The cost and difficulty of unwinding data mart proliferation
- The lack of a "voice of authority" champion for enterprise-scale initiatives
- Economic and external factors in the aftermath of two recessions and business downturns

Let's briefly look at each of the above in the context of not only what has occurred in the past but also which EBI/EDW program managers need to be aware of, even for brand new initiatives.

## Immature Technology

At the dawn of the modern BI/DW era, relational database management systems (RDBMSs) were still very much a relatively new technology. RDBMSs began appearing in the research community in the mid-1970s, and started becoming commercially available in the late 1970s and early 1980s with products from Oracle, IBM, Ingres, Digital Equipment Corporation, and other leading systems and software vendors of the day. Given the nature of RDBMS technology, significant engineering continued to go into the commercial products during the early days to enable those RDBMSs to finally be capable of supporting online transaction processing (OLTP) functionality. Specifically, substantial engineering work went into the query plan optimization necessary to provide acceptable performance for the types of database read/write access commonplace to OLTP applications and their typically normalized or lightly denormalized database schemas.

Given that data warehouses typically structure their data dimensionally (to support OLAP capabilities) rather than in a normalized manner, the types of multitable joins and other database operations commonplace in data warehousing weren't particularly well suited for the first generation or two of RDBMSs that were performance-tuned for OLTP – *particularly for large EDWs with tremendous volumes of data and hundreds or thousands of tables.* Data loading and user response times were often unpredictable at best, and very often substandard and unable to meet stated requirements.

The multidimensional technology (e.g., data cubes) developed by vendors such as IRI (Express), Arbor Software (Essbase), and Cognos (PowerPlay) as an alternative to relational-based data warehousing typically worked well up to the tens-of-gigabytes size in early product implementations, but not particularly well for the data volumes early EDW planners envisioned for their systems.

Similarly, in the extraction, transformation, and loading (ETL) space, the first generation of tools often provided a user-friendly, decently architected "shell" for the ETL packages that needed to be developed, but at the same time also required significant amounts of callout code written in SQL or another language for more complex transformation operations. Whereas today's ETL products support many different patterns through graphical interfaces and drag-and-drop usage, the earlier generation of ETL packages didn't deliver nearly the degree of productivity and overall ETL lifecycle management to which we're accustomed today.

The bottom line: whereas corporate and governmental agency strategists originally had lofty goals for the "one-stop shopping of enterprise data" envisioned with EBI/EDW, and while the high-level architectural diagrams representing these goals were relatively easy to envision and draw, that first generation of BI and data warehousing technology was actually much better suited toward smaller-scale initiatives than large, enterprise-scale efforts.

Products and tools in all aspects of BI and data warehousing have dramatically improved over the years, of course, but the legacy of that first generation of enterprise-scale efforts and the overall lack of desired success wound up resulting in companies scaling back their efforts at the enterprise level and making their next BI/DW attempts with smaller-scale initiatives (next).

## Backlash From Early EDW Failures

By the latter part of the 1990s and into the early 2000s, EDWs were "out of vogue" for most organizations. Part of the reason for this en masse downscaling of aspirations is because of the boom in competing initiatives (discussed next); however, to a large extent BI/DW proponents faced significant backlash from corporate and governmental budget holders and leaders in light of so many early EDW efforts falling far short of their originally stated objectives.

The term *data mart* came into vogue by the late 1990s: data warehousing and BI capabilities applied on a much smaller scale than their enterprise-wide predecessors. Data marts typically were built with a handful of source system feeds; significantly smaller planned user community sizes; and capabilities for reporting and data analysis limited to a single business process or a single department, or some other significantly subenterprise scope.

Data marts were typically faster and less expensive to design, build, and implement than EDWs (even on-budget, deliver-by-deadline EDW efforts), and came with inherently less overall risk than an enterprise-scale effort. Despite the scope and scale limitations of data marts versus EDWs, more and more organizations turned their data insight efforts in that direction and away from the original vision of an EDW containing the critical mass of an organization's data for reporting and BI purposes.

## Many Competing Enterprise Initiatives (and the Impact of Packaged Software)

At the same time that the first generation of EBI/EDW efforts was coming up short, the mid- and late 1990s saw the dramatic rise of:

- Enterprise resource planning (ERP) packages from SAP, Oracle, PeopleSoft, Baan, and other vendors – many in response to the looming Y2K situation
- Customer relationship management (CRM) systems from Siebel, Vantive, E.piphany, and other vendors that hallmarked a new era of sales force automation (SFA), call center management, and attempts to better understand and manage the entire customer life cycle
- A new generation of supply chain management (SCM) capabilities
- The commercialization of the Internet and the birth of eCommerce

At any given point from about 1996 to 2000, almost every single company and governmental agency found themselves deluged with significant, expensive, and resource-consuming development efforts in all of the above disciplines – at the same time they were trying to cope with so many less than successful EBI/EDW results. In concert with so many organizations shifting their allegiances to embrace the data mart (vs. data warehouse) concept, most packaged software included starter kits (data models, scripting or graphical user interfaces, etc.) for reports based on their underlying transactional data.

The result: most organizations wound up steadily building out a federation of independent, nonintegrated data marts that *as an aggregate* provided the types of reporting and data-driven insights sought after from earlier EBI/EDW efforts.

The catch: because of the lack of master data and common business rules across these many data marts, the quest for a "single version of the truth" from reports and BI was typically unachievable. Customer and sales data could often be found in dozens of data marts; the same can be said for product data and many other key subject areas. Even relatively simple reports (e.g., "how many stores did we have at the end of this quarter versus the end of the same quarter last year?") coming out of different data marts often produced very different results when they should have been the same.

Still, organizational leaders just gritted their teeth, sighed, and grudgingly accepted the fact that the lack of "a single version of the truth" was an acceptable price given all that had to be accomplished in ERP, CRM, and eCommerce to (1) deal with Y2K; (2) figure out what to do about this new phenomenon called the Internet; and (3) keep pace with what their competitors were doing in all of these areas.

## "The Need for Speed"

With regards to keeping pace with competitors (mentioned in the previous section), the typical 18- to 36-month duration of early EBI/EDW initiatives became simply unacceptable by the late 1990s. Longer-duration software development methodologies such as "Waterfall" were increasingly viewed as stodgy and outdated, and organizations began to adopt newer development approaches that were hallmarked by iterative, short-duration phases, one after another, each of which delivered actual user-facing functionality.

The typically shorter development time frame for data marts versus EDWs (described and advocated in works such as Simon, 1998) helped keep the pressure on organizations to maintain a focus on the former rather than on the latter.

## Individual Business Unit BI Often More Valued Than Enterprise BI

But what of that lack of a "single version of the truth?" What about the glaring absence of cross-functional, cross-departmental, cross-geography reports that had been promised (or at least envisioned) by early advocates of enterprise BI/DW and were nowhere to be found in the midst of data mart proliferation?

It turned out that the idea of "enterprise insights" delivered to key corporate and governmental decision makers was actually more of a nice-to-have than must-have. For many organizations, despite stated strategic direction to the contrary, "the action" was still within individual business units, individual functional departments within those business units, or sometimes even individual managers or directors themselves via what might be thought of as personal data marts.

Even organizations that embraced the concept of business process management (BPM) and proceeded to identify key cross-organizational processes and their owners often built data marts to support only individual business processes (or a small collection of closely related processes).

And so, the proliferation of independent, nonintegrated data marts continued into the 2000s.

## The Cost and Difficulty of Unwinding Fragmented Data Marts
By the mid- and late 2000s (e.g., 2005–2009):

- Data warehousing and BI technology had dramatically improved.
- Collectively we were all "smarter" about what worked and what didn't work in the BI/DW world, especially at the enterprise scale.
- A new appreciation for cross-functional, cross-geography, cross-organizational data-driven insights was increasingly found in many organizations that were tired of the difficulty – or impossibility – of pulling together and then norming information from so many different data marts.
- Enterprise systems vendors had undergone significant consolidation and expansion. Oracle purchasing Siebel and PeopleSoft (and PeopleSoft had previously purchased Vantive), for example, while SAP broadened their offerings to include CRM as well as ERP and SCM. Consequently, leading vendors themselves were now touting holistic, integrated enterprise-scale data warehousing capabilities as "something good" and achievable through their newest generation of offerings.

If an organization were starting with a clean slate in the 2005–2009 time frame, and were willing to pay attention to the body of EBI/EDW lessons learned and best practices dating back to 1989–1991, enterprise-scale successes were finally much more achievable than they had ever been.

There was one significant problem, though: almost no larger-scale organization to which EBI/EDW would be of interest was starting with a clean slate. Many years of building one independent, nonintegrated – and often overlapping – data mart had resulted in a landscape of patchwork systems, many featuring radically different technologies from one another and very few sharing common master data or business rules, that would need to be unwound and migrated into whatever new EBI/EDW capabilities would be built and delivered.

To complicate matters, many of the typical organization's data marts were closely tied to operational packaged software, and separating the transactional and reporting/data analysis functionality would not be an easy proposition.

Additionally, "spreadmarts" – spreadsheet-based data marts, most commonly built in Microsoft Excel, and each usually doing its own data acquisition – dotted the typical data mart landscape by the hundreds or even thousands. Many people at all levels of an organization relied heavily on those spreadmarts for key aspects of their respective jobs, and the idea of migrating them into an EBI/EDW system was simply unpalatable to many.

## Lack of "A Voice of Authority" Champion
Certainly, throughout the entire BI/DW era that continues today, insightful program managers, architects, strategists, and others have braved all of the aforementioned challenges and headwinds and advocated the merits of business intelligence and data warehousing at the enterprise level. However, it was rare that these BI/DW advocates carried a "voice of authority" – that is, were senior enough in their respective organizations – to overcome the inertia against enterprise-scale efforts.

The modern EBI/EDW program manager role described in Chapter 2 is intended to embody just that "voice of authority" and time will tell if those chartered with building a new generation of enterprise-scale BI/DW systems will have more success than their predecessors did.

## Postrecession Retrenchment
Finally, it's worth mentioning that amidst all of the other challenges discussed above, we've had to deal with two significant business downturns during the modern BI/DW era. For several years in the early 2000s

following the dot-com crash, the 9/11 terrorist attacks, and a flurry of corporate ethics scandals, business and governmental IT spending took a significant hit, forcing many organizations to abandon, scale back, or at least slow down their BI/DW efforts – departmental as well as enterprise-scale.

After several years of decent economic growth – years that saw significant advances in technology – the Great Recession that began in 2007–2008 caused yet another serious retrenchment in IT spending for several more years.

In both situations, anyone foresightful and courageous enough to advocate enterprise-scale efforts often found absolutely no support for the necessary investment of time, resources, and capital that was needed.

And so, true EBI/EDW success remained more the exception than the norm.

## WHY WE *CAN* BE SUCCESSFUL IN TODAY'S AND TOMORROW'S EBI/EDW EFFORTS

The Great Recession is over.

Big Data technology is increasingly being applied to classic BI and data warehousing situations, not just advanced quantitative modeling and data mining.

Are we *finally* on the brink of being able to achieve the enterprise-level BI and data warehousing successes envisioned 25 years ago? I would answer that question with a qualified "yes" based on the points made below.

### A Rich, Easily Accessible Body of Knowledge

Our collective body of knowledge about business intelligence and data warehousing continues to grow, and now more than ever BI/DW professionals have near-instantaneous access to best practices, success stories, failures (and the reasons for those failures), and much more. In the age of the Internet and mobile technology, any practitioner from an EBI/EDW program manager to a developer or tester can access almost anything he or she needs, instantaneously. Blogs, case studies, industry analyst reports, white papers, list after list of best practices and lessons learned, tips and tricks from product experts – they're all there at our fingertips.

This "speed of discovery" – *if one chooses to use it* – can play an important role in keeping everyone on an initiative on target with each and every assignment and help prevent missteps that wind up snowballing into significant problems.

## A New Generation of Game-Changing Technology

As discussed in the book's Preface, I believe that Big Data technology and a new world of data-driven analytics are a key part of this next wave of business intelligence and data warehousing – *not* a replacement and certainly not an adversary.

OLAP, dashboards, visualization, and other BI paradigms aren't going away, to be replaced by heavy-math quantitative models. Dimensional analysis of data with drill-up and drill-down capabilities will still be important to understand the "why" factor of what has happened – even if predictive analytics are, at the same time, using the same collection of data to forecast what is likely to happen in the future.

Savvy EBI/EDW professionals – including program managers – who embrace the complementary and synergistic nature of classic BI and relational technology partnering (at least for a little while) with Big Data and analytics will be well served as they tackle the enterprise-scale efforts of the future.

## Greater Appreciation for the Value of Cross-Functional Business Intelligence

Earlier in this chapter, we looked at how cross-functional, cross-organizational, cross-geography business intelligence surprisingly turned out to be "devalued" versus smaller-scope BI. And, as a result, the motivation for struggling through an enterprise initiative diminished even further in favor of smaller-scale data marts.

Today, though, this silo-type thinking is rapidly diminishing. While individual organizations and business process owners may still be rather myopic about the data-driven insights that they care about, corporate and government leaders are increasingly demanding the long-promised enterprise-level insights that have been tabled for so long.

Even those leaders who have access to broad, enterprise-scale reports and dashboards often receive those capabilities through a great deal of tedious, error-prone "under the covers" manual integration of content from many different data marts and spreadmarts. As their appetite for more and more enterprise data increases, those manual processes are becoming strained to the brink of failure.

Thus, we find new emphasis placed on consolidating and synthesizing data into a single location (physical or virtual) under whatever label might be in vogue (enterprise data warehouse or data lake or data refinery) for *mission-critical purposes*.

## Broader Appreciation for Predictive and Discovery Analytics

I made the point in the Preface that many Big Data/analytics aficionados dismiss business intelligence and data warehousing as dying disciplines. Unfortunately, over the years a corollary of sorts has been true. Whereas (at least in my view) business intelligence is best thought of as a continuum encompassing past, present, future, and hidden/unknown data-driven insights, many BI/DW practitioners of the past have dismissed data mining, statistical and quantitative analysis of data, and other "tell me what is likely to happen" and "tell me something interesting and important" functionality as something they simply didn't want to deal with. Their view was that such functionality was best handled by the "quant geeks" using SAS, SPSS, or some other type of statistical package. Essentially, it was the business intelligence and data warehousing practitioners themselves (many of them, anyway) who erected the initial lines of demarcation between what the mission of BI and data warehousing should be and what was best handled "elsewhere."

Today, though, many or even most BI and data warehousing practitioners are at least somewhat aware of Big Data, predictive analytics, and the newest generation of data mining. They are starting to appreciate the importance of a continuum of data-driven insights instantiated through well-architected, well-integrated capabilities, rather than a patchwork of data management technologies and tools.

Thus, the impetus for EBI/EDW continues to build.

## "Back on the Table" Capabilities (and New Excitement)

Nearly everyone who has attended a Big Data seminar or read a Big Data white paper has seen reference to the "three Vs" – volume, variety, and velocity. Significantly larger amounts of data – not just structured data but also semistructured and unstructured content – coupled with significantly faster access to that data for analysis purposes than ever before – are at the heart of Big Data–driven analytics.

But even when it comes to classic business intelligence uses, the "three Vs" are serving to put long-mothballed desired functionality back on the table at many organizations. Strategists and architects are (figuratively speaking) dusting off old vision statements, mission documents, and project specifications and taking a fresh look at data-driven insights that had been attempted in years past, but had failed for one reason or another.

Consequently, the excitement surrounding Big Data and analytics is certainly bleeding into the "stodgy" realm of business intelligence and data warehousing for many corporate and government strategists and leaders. Those planners and visionaries on the business and functional sides of a company or governmental agency have no intention of getting drawn into the "Big Data versus data warehousing" or "analytics versus business intelligence" dogma; they are, in the spirit of the old Hewlett-Packard advertising campaign of the 1980s, asking "What if we ..." questions seeking new, innovative ways to synthesize data to drive insights of all types across the business intelligence continuum.

## Cost Pressures on the Status Quo

Finally, as many organizations have grudgingly had to acknowledge for many years, the relative ease with which small-scale, independent, non-integrated data marts and spreadmarts can be built comes at a price – in fact, a fairly hefty price. Supporting multiple BI tools, databases, and other technology for all of those data marts takes an organization in the exact opposite direction from the pursuit of economies of scale. The internal and external personnel resources required to keep all of those systems running – not to mention tracking down an ever-increasing backlog of problem tickets, many of them of the "why doesn't this report match that report?" variety – are an expensive proposition, year after year.

Leaving aside the years-earlier EDW failures that still haunt many organizations, the following question needs to be asked:

> Would we be better off in the long run if we could swap out these patchwork landscapes of data marts that don't integrate with one another and often don't agree with one another for a new, enterprise-scale data warehouse – or whatever else you want to call it – that delivers a new generation of integrated, evolvable data-driven insights?

Nearly every organization would answer the above question with a resounding "Yes!"

## LOOKING AHEAD: THE EBI/EDW PROGRAM MANAGER

Who, then, is "on point" to lead businesses and governmental agencies out of the long-standing data wilderness and shepherd their respective organizations throughout the journey to finally realizing the promise of enterprise-scale business intelligence and data warehousing?

Chapter 2 introduces the role of the *EBI/EDW program manager*. As we will discuss, this individual – or perhaps even a team of individuals for exceedingly large efforts – must have a solid understanding of today's and tomorrow's technology and best practices and the business value that can and should be delivered from what is finally built and delivered. But the program manager is also responsible for understanding how we have arrived at this point to avoid succumbing to challenges of the past *that are still out there* but – with what we know, and all of the tools at our disposal – can and should be overcome.

## REFERENCE

Simon, A., 1998. 90 Days to the Data Mart. John Wiley & Sons, New York.

## CHAPTER 2

# The Role and Charter of the Enterprise Business Intelligence and Data Warehousing Program Manager

## CHAPTER INTRODUCTION

The enterprise business intelligence and data warehousing (EBI/EDW) program manager is *the* individual chartered with leading his or her organization through the ever-difficult effort of planning, architecting, constructing, deploying, and operating an enterprise-scale BI/DW initiative. Even for an extraordinarily large initiative that requires more than one program-level leader/manager, one individual should be designated as the lead program manager, ultimately responsible for the success of the effort.

Many organizations that have successfully navigated the difficulties of EBI/EDW in the past have had those efforts led by an individual whose job description was very similar to what is described in this chapter. Conversely, organizations that have come up short with past efforts have often entrusted the leadership to an individual who may have lacked the skills, responsibilities, and authority necessary to be successful in that always-difficult role.

Successful leadership of an EBI/EDW initiative begins with the right individual in the properly defined role, and this chapter presents a concise description of how an organization's program manager position should be defined.

## THE PROGRAM MANAGER JOB DESCRIPTION

A typical EBI/EDW program manager job description would be like the following:

1. *Lead the EBI/EDW strategic planning effort.* The program manager needs to be the center point of the entire strategic planning effort for the initiative. Many different executives, directors, and managers

from a wide variety of business and IT organizations will have a stake in the effort and will be advocating their respective priorities. Long before any development-related activities begin, the EBI/EDW program manager needs to forcefully shepherd the strategic planning process through to the point at which each of the many constituencies is satisfied to the greatest degree possible.

To accomplish this critical early stage task, the program manager needs to:

- Be respected by leaders, technologists, and others from both the business and the IT side of the overall enterprise
- Be a skilled negotiator, given the many different constituencies that need to be on board and the fact that their respective priorities will often conflict with one another
- Have a clear vision of where the EBI/EDW effort needs to head and what the future state environment needs to deliver, even as the details are being worked out among the many stakeholders
- Be willing to escalate unresolvable interpersonal or interorganizational disputes, stalemates, and other roadblocks to the most senior executive ranks in the organization when absolutely necessary

2. *Have a solid understanding of business intelligence and data warehousing technology.* In some situations, a "superstar" program manager with extraordinary management and leadership abilities *and* world-class BI/DW architecture and technology skills can be secured to lead an initiative. More often, though, a separate highly skilled EBI/EDW lead architect with deep experience and solid credentials will be a key member of the program leadership team (discussed later in this chapter) – but *not* the program manager. While some people may believe that a "professional program/project manager" with little or no business intelligence or data warehousing background at all would be perfectly acceptable as an EBI/EDW program manager, I strongly believe that even if the program manager isn't serving as the lead enterprise architect, that individual needs to have a solid understanding of BI/DW core principles, architectural concepts, and the types of technologies and products that will eventually be part of the initiative. Especially as development proceeds, the program manager needs to *personally* understand issues

that are raised about potential design flaws, integration challenges, scalability concerns, and many other topics. An EBI/EDW program manager without this personal knowledge is solely dependent on the filtered views of others, and when being "grilled" by a Chief Information Officer (CIO) or other executive will only be able to parrot back whatever he or she has been told. Certainly, the program manager will be calling on others to help address and explain issues as they arrive, but the program manager's overall stature and credibility are greatly enhanced when he or she can speak articulately about BI/DW matters as well as schedules and budgets.

I made the point in Chapter 1 that the program manager should understand the history of our collective efforts at enterprise data warehousing and accompanying business intelligence. Even though technology has certainly evolved from the early 1990s and even the early to mid-2000s, program managers need to understand the many challenges that have so often caused EBI/EDW efforts to fail in one way or another. So many of those challenges are unrelated to technology and in fact are more in the realm of human factors and/or work processes – and still exist today.

3. *Own the program budget.* The program manager will be responsible for gathering all inputs from many different sources and forming a consolidated budget for the program that will be presented, approved, and then actively managed throughout the life of the initiative. The program manager will also be responsible for taking the initial inputs from multiple underlying portfolio projects (discussed in Chapter 3) and leading the effort to look for cross-project duplication and commonality that will drive program-level economies of scale (see Chapter 4).

4. *Form the EBI/EDW team.* Rarely will the program manager be the official hiring manager for every resource – or even the majority of resources – for the entire effort. As discussed in Chapter 3, EBI/EDW efforts are often composed of a number of underlying portfolio projects that span a number of different IT and business organizations. Under the portfolio approach, individual organizations often construct their own teams that then are "rolled up" into the overall EBI/EDW program.

Sometimes in these portfolio-type situations, the EBI/EDW program is responsible for hiring and staffing the majority of the members of each of the participating teams, while in other situations the staffing rights fall to other business and/or IT organizations. Even in the latter situation, the program manager still needs to establish job descriptions, skills profiles, hire/no-hire criteria, staff/don't-staff criteria, and other aspects for each and every role that will be part of the program. The same is true if outside consultancies or systems integration firms will be used for part or all of the initiative. Essentially, the program manager needs to serve as the "Chief Personnel Officer" for the entire EBI/EDW initiative, regardless of which of the many possible organizational structures winds up applying to that particular program.

5. *Own the program schedule.* As discussed later in this chapter, I strongly recommend that the program manager *not* be the person who lives with the program/project work plans for 4–6 hours each and every workday. Someone has to take on that task, of course, and we will take a look at the recommended role of the project administrator/controller a little bit later.

   Still, even though the day-to-day work plan management should be delegated to a deputy, the program manager *does* own the overall program schedule as well as the schedules of each and every portfolio project. At any point, the program manager needs to have crystal clear insight – and be able to articulate to others – how the schedule is looking, if anything is at risk for falling behind, how personnel resources and budget are tracking for what lies ahead on the schedule, etc.

6. *Be the chief problem solver.* Whether a problem that suddenly appears is one of the technology and architecture varieties, or the sudden resignation of two key resources, or the belated acknowledgment of schedule slippages from a dependent project elsewhere in the company, the program manager is on point to get that problem resolved and keep the initiative moving forward. To quote the sign that used to adorn the desk of former U.S. President Harry S. Truman: "The buck stops here." Certainly others on the EBI/EDW team as well as perhaps from elsewhere in the organization will be called upon to solve problems that arise, but each and every one is the responsibility of the program manager to see through to some sort of resolution.

7. *Own and deliver accurate, comprehensive status reporting.* The program manager is the individual who must prepare and

deliver whatever types of status reports are required by the organization. From weekly status reports to monthly or quarterly program reviews; from short-notice, ad hoc requests to brief the organization's CxO executive team to (for government initiatives) short-notice demands from the state legislature, city council, or some other governing body for an out-of-cycle update on the program – all of these responsibilities fall to the program manager.

As discussed later in this chapter, the project administrator/controller ideally is the leadership team member responsible for collecting inputs, updating and tracking documents such as work plans and budget tracking sheets, and a host of other administrative duties. Ultimately, though, these administrative tasks are performed on behalf of the program manager so that he or she can, as required, confidently deliver a complete and accurate picture of the EBI/EDW program at any point without detracting from the leadership activities that are so essential to the program's success.

## ORGANIZATIONAL REPORTING RELATIONSHIP

Ideally, the program manager reports directly to either (see Figure 2.1):

- The Chief Data Officer (CDO), if that role exists within the organization; or
- The CIO

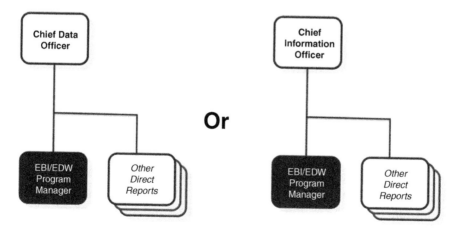

*Fig. 2.1. Recommended reporting relationships for the EBI/EDW program manager.*

The preference is for a reporting relationship to the CDO because of the data-oriented nature of that role. In fact, some might contend that the CDO should be the EBI/EDW program manager, and in some organizations that model could work. Specifically, if the CDO reports to the CIO rather than serving as a peer to the CIO, then quite possibly the primary charter of the CDO role would be to plan, build, and manage the operations of a new-generation, modern technology-based EDW.

However, the CDO – again, if that role even exists – really should be the leader of "all things data" across the enterprise, including the governance and lifecycle management of data contained within applications for enterprise resource planning (ERP), customer relationship management (CRM), supply chain management (SCM), eCommerce, and many other systems. That breadth of responsibility is a significant undertaking by itself and, in almost all situations, leaves far too little available time for what is required of the EBI/EDW program manager.

Therefore, the idea of the program manager being a key member of the CDO's staff is based on the following premise: the EBI/EDW initiative is one of the most important assets under the CDO's sphere of responsibility, and therefore a key deputy of the CDO needs to be in charge of that effort, end-to-end.

For organizations who haven't yet embraced the CDO concept, the same premise articulated in the previous paragraph applies just as fully to the CIO. CIOs inherently have a great deal of responsibility ranging from infrastructure and platforms to mission-critical applications to personnel, budgeting, and other executive management tasks. Given the importance of an upcoming enterprise-scale BI/DW initiative and the tremendous amount of personnel resources and capital that will be invested, someone with the trust of the CIO needs to be that "buck stops here" individual for the EBI/EDW effort.

Other reporting relationships may work as well. Some companies have adopted a CxO model on the IT side where the CIO is responsible for traditional CIO-type matters such as platforms and infrastructure, while the Chief Technology Officer (CTO) holds responsibility for not just evaluating and recommending new technologies but also implementing systems using those new technologies. In this case, the EBI/EDW program manager should report directly to the CTO.[1]

Some companies still have a model where the CIO reports not to the CEO but rather to either the Chief Financial Officer (CFO) or Chief Operating Officer (COO). In these situations, given the business value focus of an EBI/EDW effort, it would be highly desirable for the program manager to report not to the CIO but rather to either the CFO or the COO – highly desirable, but also highly unlikely. Still, this model is another one that would actually yield significant business visibility and (hopefully) buy-in to the EBI/EDW effort and help counteract continuing "shadow IT" data mart proliferation.

Regardless of which one of the above-referenced reporting models an organization winds up implementing, the key point is that the program manager needs to be a senior-level person – at least Director-level, perhaps even a Vice President – with that all-important "seat at the table" to compete for resources, budget, and other necessities on behalf of his or her program.

What does *not* work well is when the program manager is a level or two – or three – below the CIO, CDO, or some other CxO. Figure 2.2 illustrates an *undesirable* and almost certainly ineffective reporting relationship.

So far down the IT organizational chain, the program manager will inevitably find himself or herself buffeted by and helpless to authoritatively counteract interorganizational politics that in turn are driven by competing priorities.

## THE PROGRAM MANAGEMENT TEAM

On the other side of the reporting relationship picture, the program manager should have at least two roles reporting directly *and exclusively* to him or her. Further, a number of likely dotted-line relationships also come into play. Figure 2.3 illustrates this model.

---

[1] Other companies reverse the CIO/CTO roles, with the CIO being in charge of "information-related activities" while the CTO handles "technology-related matters" such as computer platforms, networks, etc. In that case, the EBI/EDW program manager would best report to the CIO, as described earlier.

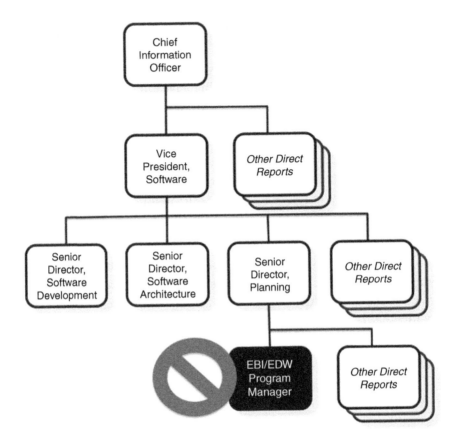

*Fig. 2.2.  Ineffective reporting relationship for EBI/EDW program manager.*

## The Program Architect

As mentioned earlier in this chapter, the program architect serves as the chief technologist for the entire initiative. The individual filling this role is responsible for evaluating technologies and products, determining and enforcing standards, architecting the models to be used to exchange control and data among various components, and most everything else technology- and architecture-related. Even though the program manager does need to be technology- and architecture-savvy, the program architect – who reports to the program manager – is the "voice of authority" for all technology and architecture matters. Essentially, this individual serves as the CTO at the program level.

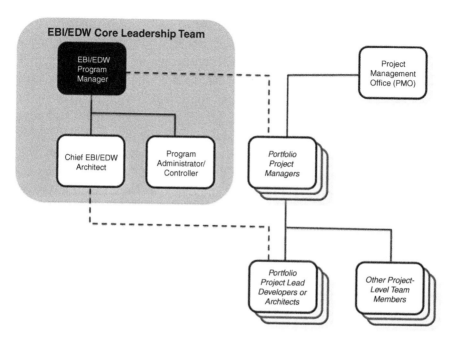

*Fig. 2.3. The EBI/EDW program management leadership team.*

The program architect will be the one who will, for example, lead the effort to determine the role of a Hadoop-based Big Data engine in the architecture. Should the EDW be Hadoop-based? Solely or alongside relational technology? What vendor distribution(s) would be best suited for this particular program, and why? These are the types of questions that fall to the program architect – and which need to be articulated *and thoroughly understood* by the program manager.

As depicted in Figure 2.3, the chief architect should ideally have a dotted-line manager–subordinate relationship with the lead technologist on each EBI/EDW portfolio project. In most cases, that lead designer/ developer or (for larger projects) project-level architect will report to his or her project manager for day-to-day direction. However, it should be the responsibility of the chief architect for the entire EBI/EDW program to coordinate the activities of each of those individuals, to ensure that they are adhering to the architectural direction and standards of the entire program, to approve variances from program-level standards when absolutely necessary, to troubleshoot particularly difficult development problems or tools issues, and so on.

## The Program Administrator/Controller

Earlier in this chapter it was mentioned that while the program manager owns responsibility for the program schedule, it's not desirable for that individual to spend hours each day with a stack of project work plans, budget tracking spreadsheets, and other materials. Certainly, all of those artifacts are immutably important to the effective management and governance of the EBI/EDW program. But tasking the program manager – the program *leader* – with so much of an administrative burden will inevitably and adversely impact the degree of oversight and hands-on leadership that the program manager must deliver from the first day of the program onwards.

Large, mission-critical projects often have a project administrator or project controller assigned to the leadership team. This individual holds the responsibility of being the "Chief Administrative Officer" for that project. He or she is the one who lives and breathes the details of the project work plan, who tracks the budget from week to week, who collects many different inputs for the weekly status report or monthly program review, and so on.

In the case of the EBI/EDW initiative, the administrator/controller function occurs at the program level, reporting directly to the program manager. Individual portfolio projects are, of course, tasked with handling their own project work plans, budget tracking, and status reporting. But regardless of whatever other communications channels and reporting requirements exist within the organization, all of those artifacts from each portfolio project need to be accessible to the program administrator/controller, who then must consolidate all of that content at the program level on behalf of the program manager.

## Portfolio Project Managers

In Chapter 3, we will look at the portfolio project approach to building an EDW environment. In many cases, the actual development teams will fall under a company-wide centralized software development organization; sometimes they may report to various development groups organized along geographic lines (North America Software Development, Europe Software Development, Central and South America Software Development, etc.), and in other cases, they may even be housed within specific business units who have control of developing the systems and capabilities that they will use. The point is that in many EBI/EDW efforts, the program manager will *not* be the one with solid-line responsibility for all of the underlying data modeling, ETL design and development, BI development, testing, quality assurance (QA), etc. Instead, those individual project managers will likely report to some sort of Project Management Office (PMO) that in turn is part of the overall application development function for the organization.

Regardless of whatever distributed development model is in place, the manager of each project within the EBI/EDW portfolio needs to have a dotted-line reporting relationship with the program manager. This way, the program manager can coordinate activities across projects, share best practices from one project that can benefit another that is struggling, stay on top of whether interproject dependencies are proceeding as planned or if trouble is on the horizon, and so on.

## WHEN A MULTILAYERED PROGRAM MANAGEMENT TEAM IS NECESSARY

Occasionally, an EBI/EDW initiative will be so large, complex, and distributed that a *team* of program managers is required. Initiatives that span multiple brands or multiple geographies – or perhaps both – may often be best suited by having multiple program managers as part of the leadership team. An example is depicted in Figure 2.4. Presume that a global EBI/EDW initiative will span 35–40 underlying portfolio projects across three geographic regions within a multinational corporation: North America; Europe, Middle East, and Africa (EMEA); and Asia Pacific (APAC).

In this situation, the span of control burden for a single program manager would likely be too great. In response, a multilayered program management model may be effective where:

- A group of three program managers – one for each global geographic region – is designated.
- One of those program managers (North America, in this case) is designated as the lead program manager, and the other two are technically subordinate to the lead. In reality, though, the three

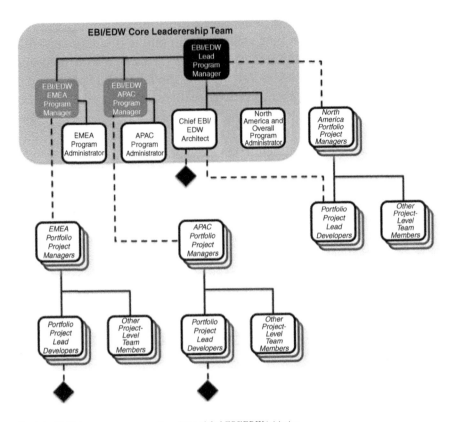

*Fig. 2.4. Multiple program managers for a large global EBI/EDW initiative.*

should form a program management triumvirate – sort of "program management by committee" but with one of them *definitively and immutably* designated as the lead.

- Each of the geographic program managers holds the dotted-line reporting relationships with the portfolio project managers within his or her respective region.
- There should only be one program architect. In this example, that individual happens to be in North America but nothing prohibits that role from being filled in any of the other geographies. Regardless of where that program architect resides, he or she will report to whomever is the lead program manager.
- Each of the program managers should have an individual program administrator/controller for work plans, budget tracking, status reporting, and other administrative functions within that geography.

Whichever one of those roles is housed in the geography where the overall program lead is, that person also serves as the administrator/controller for the overall program.

Several other points are worth noting about program management for very large EBI/EDW efforts:

- The example in Figure 2.4 shows three different geographies. The delineation could also be along brands or lines of business, government agencies, or any other relevant demarcation.
- Nothing prevents exceptionally large initiatives from having assistants or subordinates for some of these roles. For example, the program architect could have several direct reports: perhaps one for ETL and data management technology, and another for BI and analytics. Or a program administrator/controller could have someone to assist with project plans and budgeting and a separate assistant for status reporting. As long as the body of work is well orchestrated with clear lines of reporting and authority, additional members of the overall leadership team may be added as necessary.

## LOOKING AHEAD: THE PROJECT PORTFOLIO

Throughout this chapter we have referenced the idea of the "project portfolio." What exactly does that mean? Chapter 3 explores the concept of building an EBI/EDW environment through an underlying portfolio of well-coordinated projects.

# Building the EBI/EDW Program's Initial Project Portfolio

## CHAPTER INTRODUCTION

Because of the breadth of the typical enterprise business intelligence and data warehousing (EBI/EDW) initiative, it's very likely that a number of underlying projects will come together in an orchestrated manner to build out the EBI/EDW environment over a period of several years. In this chapter we look at how to build the program's portfolio of underlying projects – in fact, several different alternatives with one of those recommended above the others. We then look at fleshing out the initial pass at the portfolio with "metadata" for each project such as budgetary estimates, lists of the relevant stakeholders (as well as potential adversaries), the delta from the current state, and the incremental future value after successful delivery.

Before proceeding, we should state that it's highly recommended that an EBI/EDW program be divided into multiple underlying projects, rather than treated as a single "megaproject." By the time the typical EBI/EDW effort is scoped and resources are assigned, you will typically be looking at a resource pool of anywhere between 50 and 100 individuals filling roles such as business analysts, ETL/ELT developers, data modelers, OLAP developers, testers, change management specialists, and so on. In fact, for extremely large multigeography, multibrand EBI/EDW initiatives – the type that require a program management team rather than an individual program manager (see Chapter 2) and that involve significant amounts of data conversion and migration that can be "factory-ized" – you may be looking at teams up to 200 individuals or even more. Further, the activities of various resource groups will overlap others at some point and be sequential at others. For example, one team may spend six months working on a specific body of work related to sales data and classic BI, and then spend the next six months focusing on human resources data and retention-focused predictive analytics.

While it's not impossible to treat an EBI/EDW effort as a single mega-project with all of the underlying activities performed by various teams under the direction of a collection of team-level leaders, the breadth of functionality we will explore in this chapter is typically better suited for delivery through a portfolio of multiple interrelated projects over time. Now let's take a look at how to construct that portfolio.

## IDENTIFYING THE PROGRAM'S PORTFOLIO OF PROJECTS: ALTERNATIVES AND RECOMMENDATIONS

Over the years, EBI/EDW initiatives have constructed their project portfolios in one of several ways:

1. *IT-driven* – When the primary focus of an initiative has been to build an enterprise data warehouse, often with a philosophy of "if we build it, they will come (to use it)," the underlying projects have often been organized around various aspects of technology. For example, Figure 3.1 illustrates a typical IT-focused project portfolio consisting primarily of efforts related to data.

   The primary challenge to this approach is that it is *so* IT-focused that very often business organizations with desperate, time-sensitive needs for reporting, BI, and analytics will often bypass the EBI/EDW effort and continue to build out siloed systems. In a vacuum and without real-world pressures on time, budget, and time to business value, an EBI/EDW environment can certainly be built out in the manner depicted in Figure 3.1. Over the years, though, this particular manner of constructing the portfolio of underlying projects has often come up short.

2. *Source application-focused* – A second approach is to identify the key source systems from which data will almost certainly be needed for reporting and BI purposes, and to build the portfolio around a collection of projects tied to data acquisition from each of those source systems. Figure 3.2 depicts this approach.

   As with the first approach, this second approach also tends to be EDW-focused with the majority of the work in each underlying project focusing on data modeling, business rules for data synthesis, master data management (MDM), ETL, and so on. Likewise the challenges are much the same as with the first approach, particularly the lack of business buy-in for what is often – perhaps

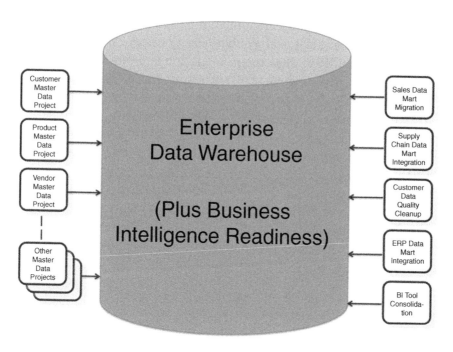

*Fig. 3.1. The IT-focused approach to constructing the EBI/EDW project portfolio.*

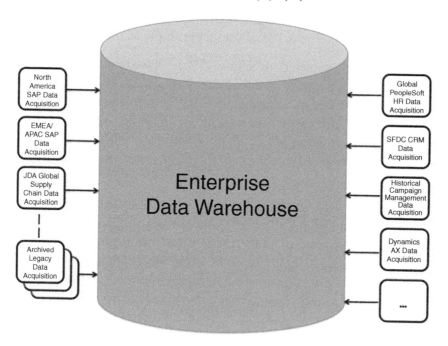

*Fig. 3.2. The source system-driven approach to constructing the EBI/EDW project portfolio.*

unfairly – perceived as an IT-dominant initiative with significantly less emphasis on timely and regular delivery of new data-driven insights. Indeed, even when report migration and/or reconstruction of source systems reporting (e.g., reports produced from SAP via ABAP and/or BW) are part of the scope, critical new functionality in analytics or even rudimentary OLAP is often secondary to the data-focused activities.

3. *BI process/functionality-driven* – A third approach is to construct the EBI/EDW portfolio around identified business intelligence-focused processes and functionality. (Recall in the *Preface* that for purposes of this book we define "business intelligence" as representing the entire continuum of data-driven insights from basic reporting to – and including – model-driven predictive analytics and other data mining capabilities.)

By focusing the body of work primarily on business-facing capabilities and even analytically focused applications, the EBI/EDW effort is established as a business-focused initiative rather than an IT-oriented one. Stakeholders can easily see what will be delivered if and when the effort is successful, and can do so in terms of their respective business processes and specific insights associated with each one. Figure 3.3 illustrates an example of this approach.

The approach depicted in Figure 3.3 is, based on this author's experience, the preferred way to construct the EBI/EDW project portfolio. Essentially, key stakeholders – executives, process owners, and others – around the enterprise "opt in" to the initiative, rather than finding themselves "dragged in" simply because they have been told that a new EDW will be built that will subsume existing data from existing systems.

Note that in Figure 3.3 the lines are bidirectional (arrows at both ends), whereas in Figures 3.1 and 3.2 the one-way direction of the lines indicates that the focus was on data acquisition for purposes of building the EDW. In Figure 3.3, the types of business functionality depicted in the outside boxes are typical of applications and business processes in which transactional/operational and reporting/analysis functions and activities are interwoven. Essentially, Figure 3.3 shows a representative set of portfolio projects that would:

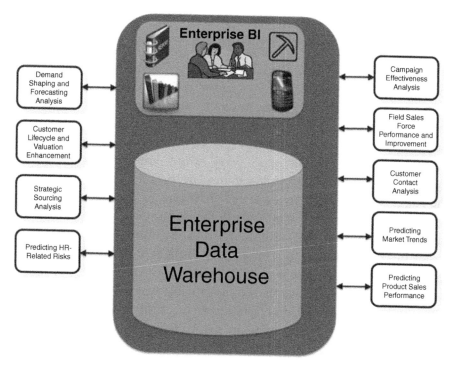

*Fig. 3.3. The BI process-driven approach to constructing the EBI/EDW project portfolio.*

- Be built by individual teams
- Be hallmarked by deep subject matter expertise on each effort
- Deliver substantial data-driven insights and business value to their respective stakeholders and constituencies
- Progressively build out specific subsets of the EBI/EDW environment
- Set the stage for cross-functional, cross-organizational data-driven insights by virtue of the end product within the EBI/EDW environment resulting from each of these individual efforts

Note also that in Figure 3.3 the portfolio projects are "all over the map" representing sales, marketing, HR, supply chain, product management, customer relations, and other organizations (vertical view) and business processes (horizontal view). This manner of building the EBI/EDW system may seem haphazard, scattershot, and a recipe for an end product that is a far cry from what a well-architected environment should look like. In reality, this process-focused, "opt-in" approach helps build the environment in a manner that is most conducive and appealing to a broad set of constituencies across the enterprise.

Will there be "holes" in the EBI/EDW environment as a result of following this approach rather than, for example, identifying all key source systems, existing data marts, master data subjects, etc.? The answer: almost certainly – but that is *not* a deal-breaker or even necessarily a bad thing. Think of the resulting EBI/EDW environment as a jigsaw puzzle that can be built in any number of ways, by any number of people working on the same puzzle. Even if people – teams – are "working around the edges" and initially disconnected from one another, at some point along the timeline of the effort interlocking touchpoints occur with increasing frequency and, eventually, a critical mass of whatever that jigsaw puzzle's picture is starts to appear. But along the way they are all working on the same jigsaw puzzle, and doing so together; they *know* what the jigsaw puzzle is supposed to look like when it's eventually finished, and there is enough coordination among individuals or teams that they know roughly how far apart to space the sections they're working on, how to parcel out individual pieces based on what part of the puzzle they most likely fit based on what they look like, and so on.

*Unlike* a jigsaw puzzle, though, an EBI/EDW environment does *not* have to be 100% complete to be considered a successful effort. Stated another way: pieces can and often will be missing and the picture is still "good." The "market economy" nature of most organizations allows for some amount of freedom to either join in some enterprise-scale initiatives or go one's own way. Unlike the corporate telephone and e-mail systems or the governmental agency's payroll system for its 15,000 employees, failure of a given organization or business process owner to participate in the building of and then using an EBI/EDW environment is *not* a showstopper. However, by constructing and delivering early successes for early adapter organizations and business processes, others who initially are more reluctant to participate may come to see *this* EBI/EDW effort as different from those that came before and actually the preferred path rather than going it alone.

Corporations and governmental agencies do need to make it somewhat difficult for individual organization executives or business process owners to continue to drag their feet and go it alone when it comes to managing data and delivering insights in a holistic manner rather than continuing with old-fashioned, silo-based thinking. Some organizational cultures are built around being early adapters with participation in enterprise-level initiatives being highly valued. Others are on the opposite end of the spectrum.

In fact, some upcoming initiatives such as several of those depicted in Figure 3.3 (demand shaping and forecasting, customer lifecycle and valuation enhancement, predicting product sales performance, etc.) are so "enterprise critical" that they may need to be "drafted" into the EBI/EDW effort in the event their key executives and stakeholders aren't willing participants. That's a call for the CxO executive ranks in the company to make.

Another key point: the initial take on the EBI/EDW project portfolio should be thought of as just that – initial. As the portfolio gets fleshed out, additional projects may well find their way into the mix, especially if there is a critical gap in the data landscape that *cannot* be left empty (referring to our jigsaw puzzle analogy). For example, as the refinement of the portfolio proceeds as we will see in Chapter 4, it may come to light that a new external source of competitor data is available that will greatly enhance product market share forecasting, and in turn will directly influence key pricing and distribution decisions. Or it may be discovered that several business unit data marts almost nobody knew about are critical pieces to the next generation of integrated demand shaping and forecasting, and thus need to be subsumed into the EBI/EDW environment.

Finally, how can this "market economy" approach to planning, building, and deploying an EBI/EDW capability be successful? It starts with a strong, visionary, and politically savvy program manager, as we looked at in Chapter 2.

## THE PROJECT PORTFOLIO "METADATA"

Once the initial portfolio has been constructed, the program manager needs to lead the effort to define the "metadata" for each of those projects, which will include:

- *An initial budgetary estimate for that project* – An enterprise-scale BI/DW initiative is not simply the sum of all of its underlying parts (i.e., portfolio projects). As we will discuss in Chapter 4, economies of scale exist that *should* make the EBI/EDW environment less expensive to construct than if each of its portfolio projects were constructed as a single, stand-alone effort with "looser" interfaces to other components. However, at the stage of building the initial portfolio, economies of scale and elimination of overlap should be set aside for the time being. Each project should be initially budgeted as if it were actually a stand-alone effort; so if our example demand shaping and forecasting analysis application required master data sets for customer, product, geography, markets, competitors, and several other subject areas, the initial budget estimate should reflect each of those MDM subject areas needing to be built as part of the project.

Why? For one reason, project budgetary estimates can be constructed more rapidly by their respective project managers than if they need to get together and decide which project might be building out the new product master that others will share, who might be doing the same for the new global customer master, and so on. These types of "who builds what" decisions tend to be rather fluid as the EBI/EDW project portfolio evolves, and rather than send project managers and their respective business and IT stakeholders into "early negotiations and empire-building mode," initial budgetary estimates can simply reflect a "we need to do it all" focus – at least for the first cut at the budget.

A second reason is that executive sponsorship and ongoing support for an EBI/EDW effort can be enhanced by *first* showing a "build them independently" budgetary estimate versus subsequent passes in which economies of scale surface and overlapping, duplicate efforts are eliminated. Keep in mind that many executives on the business side don't have a full understanding of the nature of shared IT components; to them the EBI/EDW environment may simply reflect the sum of the individual parts as represented by the composite project portfolio. A great deal of executive buy-in and ongoing support may be gained from showing an initial sum-of-the-parts portfolio budget of, say, $12 million but after allocating the build-out of various master data subject areas to individual projects and eliminating duplicate effort (not to mention the inevitable apples-vs.-oranges master data mismatches), the program-focused budget comes in $3 million lower at $9 million. As the program proceeds and the inevitable challenges surface, the financial uplift from a program-level effort rather than a collection of individual efforts should be a constant reminder for key CxOs to proactively resolve challenges escalated to them rather than dismiss them as "an IT matter," often leaving the initiative to succumb to otherwise resolvable problems.

- *The stakeholders across the enterprise* – No doubt the key stakeholders for various pieces of the initiative will be known to various parties involved in the EBI/EDW effort, but at this stage a composite list of stakeholders should be formulated along with the various pieces of the environment that are of primary or secondary interest to them. Essentially, the program manager needs to have a complete, up-to-date picture of "who are the players" and what particular interests each one has with the end result.

- *The potential adversaries across the enterprise* – Although the idea of compiling an "enemies list" may seem draconian, the program manager cannot afford to be naïve about threats of all types to the success of his or her program. Certainly, the program manager should *not* prepare a program charter document and accompanying PowerPoint presentation that contains a list of the portfolio projects, the initial (and then revised) budget for the program, the overall timeline and phasing – and then the list of identified adversaries who represent threats to the program! Hopefully the list in a given situation is small enough – three or four individuals at most – to be committed to memory by the program manager (and perhaps quietly discussed with his or her most trusted members of the leadership team). Even if the program manager feels the need to create a log of actions by those potential adversaries "for future use," he or she should *not* put such a list out on the program SharePoint site or common program directory. A *password-enabled* word processing file or spreadsheet, or perhaps encrypted mobile phone notes, would be the better vehicle for such documentation – at least until it becomes necessary to compile a body of evidence to escalate to the program sponsors and executive leadership.

- *If/how the business functionality is being performed today* – As the EBI/EDW planning and strategizing continues, challenges or at least questions of the "we already do that" variety are bound to appear.

Certainly, much of the business functionality that will become a key part of the EBI/EDW environment will indeed exist. In many or even most cases, though, the current state will be found to lack key functionality that is intended to be part of the EBI/EDW-driven future state. For example, plenty of reports may be produced today that indicate various slices and views of how the company's field sales force is performing (again referring to Figure 3.3). However, the envisioned future state will not be hallmarked by a monthly, e-mailed collection of a dozen or so static reports but rather a comprehensive collection of productive reports, self-service BI with full user-driven "slice and dice" functionality, as well as a robust set of analytical models designed to augment past performance reporting with data-driven predictions about future performance.

Building a comprehensive, across-the-board picture of the delta between the current state and the future state will be very important as the initiative moves forward and program and project challenges surface, followed soon by the inevitable "why are we rebuilding what we already have?" questions. It will be very important for the program manager to demonstrate that the envisioned and planned future state is *not* the same as the current state.

- *What alignments exist between the EBI/EDW initiative and other significant enterprise-scale business initiatives* – In Simon (2014) I discussed how an organization's overall enterprise data management road map takes inputs from and needs to be aligned with key business initiatives at the enterprise level. Essentially, the greater the need for consolidated, well-integrated data for a business initiative, the greater the importance of a well-governed road map for data across the enterprise (including transactional systems) and supporting processes such as data quality, help desk, etc. Examples include global cross-brand, cross-geography strategic sourcing; lean supply chain initiatives; enterprise systems rationalization and consolidation; heightened risk management and mitigation; and others.

The same is true for an EBI/EDW initiative. Any enterprise-scale business initiative requires an enterprise approach to data management and the business intelligence associated with that data.

By identifying key alignments to specific planned projects within the EBI/EDW portfolio as early as possible, additional support from business executives and stakeholders who might not otherwise have any involvement in the EBI/EDW effort can be secured.

## LOOKING AHEAD: REFINING THE EBI/EDW PROJECT PORTFOLIO

Constructing the initial EBI/EDW portfolio – the list of projects and the "metadata" associated with each – is a formidable task. The portfolio planning work is far from completed, though, and in Chapter 4 we will look at the "end game" for finalizing the body of work necessary to build and deploy the EBI/EDW environment.

As a side note, this initial stage is also a good way for a company or governmental agency to get an early look at whether the designated program manager does indeed "have the right stuff" for the tasks that lie ahead. A program manager who authoritatively leads his or her organization through this effort on schedule and produces a sound, defensible portfolio of capabilities has passed his or her first test. Conversely, someone who struggles with this initial planning-stage set of activities will inevitably struggle with what will follow, and a change may be necessary.

## REFERENCE

Simon, A., 2014. Modern Enterprise Business Intelligence and Data Management: A Roadmap for IT Directors, Managers, and Architects. Morgan Kaufmann Publishers Waltham, MA.

## CHAPTER 4

# Putting the Finishing Touches on the EBI/EDW Program's Project Portfolio

## CHAPTER INTRODUCTION

Accomplishing the body of work for the enterprise business intelligence and data warehousing (EBI/EDW) project portfolio discussed in Chapter 3 is a daunting task and will require a great deal of effort and understanding of the organization's strategic direction. However, determining the initial set of portfolio projects and their "metadata" is hardly the end of the work.

This chapter discusses what comes next for the program portfolio at the planning stage that must be successfully accomplished before development should begin. Some of the tasks might actually overlap some early "experimental" development work: for example, a proof-of-concept pilot effort to validate certain leading-edge architectural concepts before fully committing the entire initiative to that architectural direction. But for the most part, the activities described in this chapter should be thought of as a prerequisite to full-scale development. The list includes:

- Identifying overlapping capabilities and potential economies of scale
- Prioritizing the list of portfolio projects
- Finalizing the program's architecture
- Updating and finalizing the program budget
- Risk mitigation and contingency planning
- Preparing the program time line and project work plans
- Conducting the *Critical Design and Schedule Review* (CDSR)
- Securing buy-in and sponsorship

## IDENTIFYING OVERLAPPING CAPABILITIES AND POTENTIAL ECONOMIES OF SCALE

Chances are that after the initial project portfolio is defined, the program management team will, on analyzing the details of the projects, find that (e.g.):

- Seven of the twelve projects in the portfolio require a complete set of customer master data.
- Eight of the twelve projects in the portfolio require a complete set of product master data.
- Three of the twelve projects in the portfolio require a complete set of vendor master data.
- Four of the twelve projects in the portfolio share many of same dashboard-based key performance indicators (KPIs) planned for delivery to end users.

The above list may include many more items. Recall that in Chapter 3, I advised that during the *initial* construction of the project portfolio the program management team *not* attempt to rationalize overlapping uses of master data or common user-facing functionality across the projects. Those rationalization and consolidation efforts do, of course, need to occur at some point during the initiative's planning efforts – and now is the time.

Let's look at the example in our first bullet point: 7 of the 12 projects in the portfolio require a complete set of customer master data. Presuming that's the case, two different approaches might be pursued:

1. A *customer master data* project might be added to the earliest activities in the portfolio to design a common data model for the customer master; produce a consolidated, cross-organizational, and cross-functional set of business rules applying to the customer master; bring the customer source data into the data warehousing environment and continue to do so to keep the customer master current; and so on. The seven identified projects then use this set of customer master data *rather than each creating its own.*

Or, alternatively:

2. One of the seven projects could be identified as being responsible for building the customer master on behalf of the entire EBI/EDW

program, and will be designated to occur early in the sequence of portfolio projects so that at the points in the respective work plans of the other six when each one requires customer master data, that particular master data is ready to use as needed.

While the first alternative (a new customer master data project) might sound similar to the portfolio construction approach depicted in Figure 3.1 – an approach we declared as not particularly desirable for modern EBI/EDW systems – we actually have a different scenario in today's Big Data era. Previously, the up-front work and build-out of a customer master data set intended for program-wide use might take (e.g.) 6–9 months and cost upwards of $1 million including master data management (MDM) software – yet *initially* produce little or no user-facing business value. Such an effort would be squarely within the IT realm, and only on the *eventual* development and deployment of BI capabilities would the customer master begin to deliver user-facing business value – no matter how well it was architected or how well the business rules had been constructed to satisfy the needs of the entire enterprise.

Today, the bulk of source system-provided customer data – which in most cases would be coming from a number of different transactional systems as well as perhaps even from external data sources – could be quickly "dumped" (not in a bad way) into a Big Data engine. Then, as business rule creation, data definitions, and all the rest of the necessary work occur using the power of, say, a Hadoop-based solution, the Big Data-driven analytics could *also* mine through all of that data – even in raw, unfiltered form – and look for patterns and other insights that in turn can be delivered as *hypotheses* to data scientists and others within the organization.

To classic BI/data warehousing professionals, this idea may seem backwards – essentially, mining a first-level staging area filled with unprocessed, even "dirty" data and inadvisably attempting to produce valuable insights from that data before any sort of quality assurance or other governance is applied. But if these Big Data-driven insights are treated as hypotheses – that is, something to look into, now or at some point later when the data is eventually transformed and unified – but critical business decisions are *not yet* made until further analysis occurs against "better" versions of the data, interesting data-driven insights (albeit preliminary ones) can be produced quickly and continue all throughout the necessary work to create the uniform set of customer master data.

The second alternative – assigning one of the seven projects that can occur early enough in the overall sequence to be responsible for the customer master for all the others – is sort of a "shared development services" type of approach. In theory, this approach can work with very strong program management that identifies and carefully tracks interproject dependencies. The risk, of course, is that if the designated customer master-building project runs into trouble, those problems will likely ripple through the entire portfolio. So if at all possible, a lower-risk, lower-complexity project should be selected as the one that takes on the building of the customer master on behalf of the entire program. The same is true of the product master, vendor master, and common KPIs – anything that is overlapping across multiple portfolio projects and that, if handled properly, can drive program-level economies of scale.

Which of the two approaches is preferable? Until the Big Data era came along, I would have recommended the second approach: the designated project acting as a shared development service on behalf of the entire program. With the advent of the sequence of activities described for the first alternative, though, the organization can began realizing business value through data-driven insights very early in the program life cycle and earlier than following traditional BI/DW sequencing. Either can work but if Big Data technology has been selected to be part of the overall architecture (see Chapter 8 for further discussion), program managers should strongly consider the first alternative.

## PRIORITIZING THE LIST OF PORTFOLIO PROJECTS

Continuing the discussion from the previous section, if a given project has indeed been selected to build a specific set of master data on behalf of the entire program, that stated program direction definitely needs to be factored into the sequencing and prioritization of the portfolio projects. But beyond simple predecessor–successor dependencies, how should the relative priorities and sequencing within project portfolio occur?

The program manager needs to take a number of different factors into consideration as he or she leads this activity. Three factors in particular to consider include:

1. *High-priority business needs to fill gaps* – Are any projects providing specific mission-critical business insights totally absent from today's environment – and need to be available sooner than later?
2. *Data mart retirement efforts* – What projects within the EBI/EDW programs would, on successful completion, result in the decommissioning and retirement of multiple existing data marts and further result in significant cost savings through those retirements – sooner than later?
3. *Alignment with development of other applications and high-priority business initiatives* – What EBI/EDW projects are intended to provide the broad continuum of data-driven insights specifically for other in-progress efforts (e.g., a sweeping ERP upgrade and consolidation or a new enterprise-wide CRM system)?

The program manager needs to lead a number of "what-if scenario" sessions in which the portfolio projects are laid out and then sequenced and parallelized in many different combinations. The relative advantages and disadvantages of each "package" along with package-specific risks, complications, and other considerations need to be clearly identified.

Ideally, one particular packaging option will stand out clearly above all others, and be selected as the foundation of the going-forward early stage program road map. If more than one alternative percolates to the top of the list of options with no clear-cut winner, perhaps either would suffice with the other being held in reserve in case anything significant in the overall situation changes as the planning stage moves toward its conclusion.

## FINALIZING THE PROGRAM'S ARCHITECTURE

At this stage of the program planning effort, the leadership team – led by the program architect – should have a pretty good idea of the high-level program architecture. Will a Hadoop-based "data lake" serve as a supersized staging area, also usable for data exploration? Will relational database technology coexist with Big Data technology? Will one of the existing BI tools used across the enterprise be selected as the going-forward standardized platform for all of the future enterprise business intelligence delivery? Will the primary data interchange mechanism across the entire architecture follow an extract/load/transformation (ELT) paradigm rather than traditional extract/transformation/load (ETL)?

These questions – and dozens more – will have already been worked by the program architect in concert with the program manager, project-level architects and lead developers, technology strategists across the organization, and perhaps other stakeholders as well.

At this point, though, with the project portfolio starting to take shape, with a pretty good idea of the sequencing and interdependencies among various projects and their eventually delivered components, and all of the other knowledge gained thus far, the program architecture needs to be solidified.

All assumptions should be explored further and challenged, open questions to vendors that have yet to receive answers need to be pushed, tool decisions that haven't been finalized need to be closed so architectural considerations can be validated, and so on.

Additionally, leading into our next section, the initial program budget (see Chapter 3) needs to be refined and finalized to move forward, and a key contributor to that budget is being absolutely certain what products and tools – as well as development resources and required time for custom-developed architectural interfaces – will be part of the upcoming development activities.

## UPDATING AND FINALIZING THE PROGRAM BUDGET

In Chapter 3, we explored the idea of the initial program budget being created as simply the "sum of the parts" of all of the underlying projects intended to be part of the portfolio. Now, though, that budget needs to be finalized by:

- *Factoring in the impact of shared development* – If (referring back to our example earlier in this chapter) seven different portfolio projects need customer master data but one of those projects has now been designated to build the customer master on behalf of the entire program, that means that the project-level budgets for the other six can be reduced by the customer data activities (ETL/ELT, data modeling, QA, etc.) each no longer needs to perform. At the same time, though, the project that has been designated to build the common customer master likely needs to have its own budget *increased* to account for additional program-level data activities required to "ruggedize" the master data set and make it usable by not just that project but rather the entire program.

Throughout the portfolio, these interdependency-related adjustments need to be translated into the relevant budget decreases (mostly) and increases, resulting in an adjusted per-project price tag as well as a new budget for the entire program.

- *Finalizing resources on each project* – The initial per-project staffing models need to be revisited. Is the right number of resources in the right roles, at the right time, with the right level of experience for each? Does the latest thinking about the body of work for each project cause a relook at the resources and/or time lines?
- *Software and hardware costs* – With the final (or near-final) program-level architecture in place, what is the final lineup of hardware and software that will be needed, and what are the associated license and maintenance costs? Are price tags finalized? Are there any hidden costs that haven't yet been accounted for?

All of the above budget-focused activities, and any others, need to occur at this stage. Adjustments may still be forthcoming as the planning stage comes to an end, but those adjustments need to be relatively modest to avoid any "budget blast" backlash to a program that no doubt already has its share of skeptics and even adversaries around the organization.

## RISK MITIGATION AND CONTINGENCY PLANNING

A significant planning-stage activity is to develop a comprehensive risk mitigation plan and to align that plan with contingencies at various stages of the program. Because of the amount of information to convey about this activity, the topic is discussed separately in Chapter 5.

## PREPARING THE PROGRAM TIME LINE
## AND PROJECT WORK PLANS

With priorities and sequencing, project-level time lines, project interdependencies, and contingency plans (mentioned above but discussed in Chapter 5) all finalized or close to final, now is the time to consolidate all of the underlying project plans into a program-level work plan. Each individual project manager will still manage his or her own project plan, but all milestones, major levels of activity, etc., need to be rolled up into a single work plan. The program administrator/controller now steps to the forefront of the EBI/EDW initiative, ensuring that the often tedious activities occur to create an accurate picture of where the program should be at any given point in time.

While the program administrator/controller will be the one to handle the "grunt work" of creating and then regularly updating the consolidated work plan – as well as coordinating with each of the individual project managers – the program manager owns the result and is ultimately responsible for ensuring that the work plan is an accurate depiction of reality throughout the entire initiative.

## CONDUCTING THE CRITICAL DESIGN
## AND SCHEDULE REVIEW

Chances are that most or all underlying projects will follow some sort of "Agile BI" methodology. Most Agile-oriented methodologies downplay the need for comprehensive, all-hands, Waterfall-oriented walkthroughs. However, even though the underlying projects may be run Agile-like with a great deal of empowerment to teams and individuals (as long as milestones are met with the agreed-to quality deliverables), before any development work begins a comprehensive and *critical* look at all design work and scheduling needs to occur. (For purpose of this discussion and a common understanding of terminology, think of a "design" as a lower-level, more detailed look at a specific portion of the overall program architecture – essentially, "the devil in the details.")

Likewise, all of the individual work plans that have already been created need to have an equally critical, collective eye cast on them coming from the entire program team looking for potential issues, tight-timeline interdependencies with no room for error, overly optimistic assumptions, etc.

Essentially, the *CDSR* should be thought of as the final chance to catch potentially significant technology and schedule errors that for whatever reason have gone undetected. The philosophy going into the meeting and that should hold throughout is verbalizing the following *two* questions, over and over:

- "What could go wrong here?"
- "Could we do this differently and better?"

The questions aren't negative ones, and shouldn't be thought of as such. Rather the questions should be thought of as: "What could go wrong here that if we catch now, address, and adjust will help prevent extra-long hours, rework, schedule slippages, budget overruns, and even failure of the entire program?"

The program manager should lead this all-hands event, and ample time should be scheduled. Depending on the size of any particular EBI/EDW initiative, the CDSR could take anywhere from 2 to 5 days. *By no means is this an effort that should be scheduled for the typical half-day session that hallmarks so many significant business technology initiatives –* and then afterwards, when an initiative goes bad, people ask, "why didn't we identify the potential for that problem earlier?"

Ideally, the CDSR should be held in an offsite location, or at least a company location venue in which the importance of the event is emphasized, so, in other words, not a rotating series of conference rooms, two or three each day, repeatedly shuttling around because of overall conference room scheduling.

Everyone involved in the CDSR – and everyone with any role on the EBI/EDW program *should* be participating – should be grounded in the "what could go wrong here?" philosophy and be assured that raising potential issues is a "good thing" whether or not those worries ultimately prove to be a problem or not.

The program manager should be the facilitator and leader throughout – again, an opportunity for him or her to demonstrate leadership on the entire initiative – and indeed should actually verbalize the "what could go wrong here?" and "could we do this differently and better?" questions repeatedly throughout the CDSR, from the kickoff of the event to its conclusion.

## SECURING BUY-IN AND SPONSORSHIP

The end game for the EBI/EDW portfolio planning process is *securing buy-in and sponsorship* as the program moves from planning into building and delivering. Everything should be in place at this point:

- A solid architecture that has been fleshed out to significant level of detail and gone through with the proverbial fine-tooth comb.
- A revised and refined, approved budget that has achieved maximum economy of scale.
- Skilled resources are fully in place (and trained as necessary).
- Risks have been identified with mitigation and contingency plans likewise in place.

At this point, the program manager needs to secure buy-in from "everyone involved with the EBI/EDW initiative." Of course, "everyone involved" is an objective that more often than not cannot be fully achieved. Adversaries almost always exist, and even though some may be won over – or at least "sent to a neutral corner" – some will remain opposed to the effort for the duration. However, if the program manager secures buy-in from:

- An overwhelming majority of stakeholders
- Owners of related projects
- Support technologists (e.g., systems administration staff members who manage enterprise scheduling and on whom many projects are dependent to put their software into production)
- Owners of incoming market data
- Procurement specialists responsible for interfacing with hardware and software vendors

and individuals in other roles who have *any* relationship to the initiative, the EBI/EDW effort should come to be viewed as an effort that is not only widely supported but also unstoppable despite stalling tactics and other unsavory behavior.

Additionally, the executive-level sponsorship for the initiative needs to be reaffirmed by the program manager at this point. Too many large, enterprise-scale initiatives begin with statements by the COO, CFO, CIO, maybe even the CEO, and others that "this initiative is one of the most important ones we've undertaken and will transform the way we do business ...." However, as the effort proceeds and challenges of all types arise, the executive-level sponsorship that should be involved to get beyond roadblocks and deal with significant issues is nowhere to be found.

So at this point, the program manager should do whatever he or she can to secure – reaffirm – the sponsorship of the highest levels within the organization. As discussed in Chapter 7, the program-level reviews should be for the executive sponsors, not lower-ranking business and IT individuals.

And if the program manager cannot secure that continuing sponsorship? The EBI/EDW initiative can and should move forward, but all involved – especially the program manager – should be well aware that rough sailing could be ahead and if indeed that does happen, involvement by executive sponsors may not be anywhere near as active as needed.

## LOOKING AHEAD: RISK MITIGATION AND CONTINGENCY PLANNING

As noted earlier in this chapter, Chapter 5 is a "callout" for one of the key activities that needs to occur during the refinement of the program's portfolio. We will take a look at risk mitigation and contingency planning for an EBI/EDW initiative.

# Program-Level Risk Management

## CHAPTER INTRODUCTION

In the previous chapter we included identifying risks and corresponding mitigation strategies as an essential activity for finalizing the EBI/EDW project portfolio. We also mentioned that the subject was lengthy enough to be broken out into a separate chapter. In this chapter, then, we will look at some of the most significant EBI/EDW program risks including:

- Technology and architecture
- Interdependencies among components
- Apathetic and detached leadership
- Shared or part-time resources
- Budget cuts after the program begins
- New and conflicting data marts appearing
- The arrival of new stakeholders, executives, and others
- Program adversaries

## TECHNOLOGY AND ARCHITECTURE

Ever since the dawn of the business intelligence and data warehousing era, technology and architecture has had a causal relationship with the success or failure of many initiatives – especially larger, enterprise-scale ones. These factors include:

- Whether commercial software products for BI/OLAP, ETL, and other facets of solutions "actually work as advertised"
- Whether commercial software products can adequately scale from smaller solutions to enterprise ones
- Whether published or demonstration-time database performance results are reflective of real-world implementations or whether they might have been "gamed"
- Whether data interchange among components via ETL, enterprise application integration (EAI), enterprise information integration

(EII), or other paradigms works as well in actual implementations as it would seem to be based on diagram-level, predevelopment architectural work

Now, factoring Big Data into the solutions picture and being fairly early in this new era, we can add considerations such as:

- With the Hadoop-based "data lake" concept – that is, developing a "supersized staging and ODS area that will ingest 'all our data'" – how well does postingestion master data management (MDM), business rule development, and other necessary data governance activities actually fit into the construction and operations life cycle?
- What are specific areas to watch for hybrid architectures featuring Hadoop-based content alongside relational-based data?
- Are there any specific data access use cases for "OLAP on top of Hadoop" that may be especially problematic in the near term, that is, have subpar performance or response time for some reason?
- Is there a role for other Big Data solutions – for example, MongoDB, columnar databases, and other high-performance data warehousing appliances – in a given architecture and, if so, what integration concerns and unknowns might be out there?
- How mature are the new class of predictive and discovery analytical tools? Which ones are best and which ones might not be ready for bet-your-business enterprise implementations?

Undoubtedly we could come up with dozens more architecture- and technology-related questions – that is, risks – to consider. The point is that, first and foremost, program managers and program architects in particular need to be very cautious, prudent, and even skeptical as they assess core technologies, commercial products, and architectural paradigms for their program because of the inherent risks at the early stage of a new generation of solutions.

## Mitigation Strategies

To mitigate risk with regards to technology and architecture, program managers and program architects need to:

- *Seek real-world references* – Who is using a particular tool? Is their architecture similar to what you are considering? What is working? What isn't working as well as it should – or at all? How has a vendor's problem resolution been in terms of customer support, correctly identifying root causes of problems, distributing software patches and updates, etc.?

- *Have live test demonstrations (LTDs)* – Vendors need to prove their solutions, with real data in environments as close to production quality as possible.
- *Have "search and destroy" assessments of products and architectural components* – Chapter 4 discussed the concept of the *Critical Design and Schedule Review* (CDSR) during the final stages of building the program's project portfolio. Even before that stage of planning, however, the program architect needs to take the lead in approaching individual products and tools as well as the overall architecture with an "Inspector General's eye," that is, continually and persistently look for aspects that aren't well explained, look like they may not work as advertised, or are unproven in actual real-world implementations. The program architect should lead this effort but be assisted by the program manager, the lead developers from underlying portfolio projects, and even those who may not even have deep technical knowledge but who are gifted in asking the right kind of "could you please explain this in more detail?" types of questions.
- *Have architectural-level proof of concept* – Again led by the program architect but assisted by others on the EBI/EDW program, newer and less proven portions of the architecture should be tested in a contained environment, trying to prove the concepts that may look perfectly valid on high-level diagrams but for which nagging doubts exist.

Do all of the above mitigation steps take a significant amount of time? Definitely. Do they delay the start of development and implementation activities? Again: of course. But are they important enough that the program's overall risk is increased if they are *not* done thoroughly enough – or at all? Absolutely!

## "MANY MOVING PARTS" INTERDEPENDENCIES

The above section discussed interdependencies among EBI/EDW tools and products, custom-developed or out-of-the-box interfaces, data management platforms, and other components of the overall program. But what about interdependencies with other systems and applications that may also be in development in parallel, such as:

- A major ERP upgrade
- A new supply chain rationalization and consolidation effort
- Moving the company's CRM capabilities to a cloud-based provider
- A major mobile technology rollout

These types of efforts, and many others, typically have touchpoints into the EBI/EDW world. Every single one of these moving parts needs to be carefully managed for interdependencies in both schedule and architecture. Basically, the more moving parts, the greater the overall risk exposure to not only the EBI/EDW program but the other initiatives as well.

## Mitigation Strategies

The EBI/EDW program manager should be part of an *Enterprise Program Management Council* (or some other name for a *formally defined* committee of the program managers of the organization's most critical enterprise-scale initiatives). This *Council* needs to meet regularly to explore the latest status of the respective programs, their touchpoints, and potential issues that could ripple through multiple initiatives. The EBI/EDW program architect needs to likewise meet with his or her counterparts on the other initiatives, and the EBI/EDW program administrator/controller should likewise spend adequate time with those filling that role on other programs for purpose of ensuring work plans and schedules reflect reality.

## APATHETIC AND DETACHED LEADERSHIP

In earlier chapters we discussed the importance of beginning with high-profile support from a company's or governmental agency's top leadership, and then securing and ratifying that support as the planning stage concludes and moves into implementation. But what happens if that leadership support falters and fades over time?

The academic literature is filled with a body of evidence highlighting the difference in results between enterprise-scale initiatives that proceed with top management support (TMS) throughout implementation versus ones that don't (Dong et al., 2009).

A simplified predecessor–successor relationship can be stated: if *active* executive-level sponsorship and involvement continues *throughout* an initiative (i.e., support doesn't fade away following the conclusion of the planning stages and finalizing the program's project portfolio and budget), program risks are significantly minimized due to executive sponsors helping to overcome architectural difficulties, deal with resourcing issues and potential adversaries (discussed in the next two sections, respectively), and work through the many challenges that will undoubtedly arise.

## Mitigation Strategies

Chapter 7 discusses the quarterly EBI/EDW program review that should, to be most effective, involve *all* of the program's executive sponsors and stakeholders. Even beyond the quarterly review, the program manager should issue a regular report – ideally biweekly – to the executive sponsorship team. This report should present an unfiltered, unvarnished picture of the true state of the EBI/EDW program, including not only the key performance indicators (KPIs) and key operating indicators (KOIs) discussed in Chapter 6 but also enough narrative information to convey any and all risks – *as well as specifically requested actions on behalf of the executive leadership sponsors.*

## NONDEDICATED RESOURCES

A common occurrence on enterprise-level business intelligence/data warehousing efforts is to have a significant portion of the resources on various projects in "nondedicated" status, specifically:

- Development resources who "belong" to some other project or organization with full-time responsibilities but who are designated to work on some aspect of the EBI/EDW initiative on a part-time basis.
- Development resources who belong to a large pool under the direction of some sort of software factory-type structure, and who are allocated to one or more projects in any given week in a manner designed to maximize their utilization across those projects; that is, if a database administrator (DBA) is expected to be needed 20 hours/week for 2 weeks straight, then he or she will be assigned another 20 hours/week on one or more other projects to ensure a 40-hours schedule.

The risk of any nondedicated resource model is the possibility that at any given point in the program on any given project, a particular skill-set in a specific role may actually not turn out to be available. Consider the above DBA example. If some other non-EBI/EDW project to which that DBA is assigned turns out to be in trouble, that person may need to devote far more than the anticipated 20 hours that first week to that other project, meaning that that DBA needs to either (1) scale back on the allocated time for the EBI/EDW portfolio project or (2) work extra hours to accommodate both project assignments. And even if extra hours are the example, you may still run into the situation where that resource isn't available at a specific time of a specific day when work is needed to keep other activities moving forward on schedule.

## Mitigation Strategies

To the greatest extent possible, EBI/EDW program managers should try to avoid using nondedicated resources, particularly on key portions of the program and especially in the earliest stages of the overall effort. If shared resources are unavoidable, all of the underlying portfolio project managers should have contingency plans to deal with last-minute unavailability of resources. Perhaps every named resource from a common pool should have a backup also named, or perhaps outside resources from a supplemental staffing firm or systems integration company could be "on call" and available on short notice.

The program administrator/controller should also have such a comprehensive eye toward the program schedule that predefined contingency plans to vector back on schedule after a short period of time are already identified if a resource is delayed.

Essentially, if nondedicated program resources are an inevitability to an EBI/EDW program, then a well-thought-out set of backup plans to deal with last-minute unavailability of key resources should also be.

## DELAYED BUDGET CUTS

What happens when an EBI/EDW program begins with an approved budget and then 15 months into the program a budget cut suddenly appears?

Budget cuts are a fact of business and IT life. Whether caused by an overall economic slowdown or causes specific to a company (e.g., unexpected weak sales results, or the need to divert funds to a new product launch), program managers should always have an eye toward possible cutback scenarios that could play out.

## Mitigation Strategies

First, program managers should not be caught by surprise. If an EBI/EDW program manager truly has a "seat at the table" for his or her all-important initiative, then discussions leading up to the official announcement of a budget cut should fully include the program manager.

Contingency plans should be in place for various levels of budget cutbacks at various points in the program. For example, if a 10% cut were to occur at the 12-month point, then some well-thought-out set of adjustments will be the result, whereas if a 20% cut were to occur at the 12-month point, some other well-thought-out set of adjustments will be made.

If, however, a 10% cut were to occur at the 18-month point, the adjustments may well be different than those made at the 12-month point because of the different stage of the program.

The point is that like a baseball manager or football coach, the program manager should have a robust "game plan" that includes not only the road map that has been built but also a number of predetermined adjustments, even if those adjustments never come to fruition.

All adjustments, regardless of what degree of budget cut or where they may occur in the program, need to take into account all of the touchpoints from a program-level perspective. Suppose that a $1.5 million budget cut occurs, and in looking at the project portfolio the build-out of the customer and product masters together shows up as $1.5 million on the portfolio. There you have it: the perfect place to cut, right? Probably not! Absent the build-out of the customer and product masters, many other portions of the program won't be able to operate correctly without picking up the slack themselves – for additional per-project cost, of course.

Where should mandated budget cuts occur? The answer will vary from any one initiative to another but, in general, program managers should look for functional components that (1) are as compartmentalized and with as few touchpoints as possible with other parts of the program or other enterprise systems; (2) aren't on the "insights we must have *now*" list; and (3) could be mothballed and then quickly revived with as little impact on the rest of the program as possible.

## NEW AND CONFLICTING DATA MARTS

One of the primary objectives of an EBI/EDW initiative is usually to move an organization away from a fragmented patchwork of standalone, organization- or function-specific data marts. Part of the planning process is to identify data marts that should and will be decommissioned on successful delivery of some portion of the EBI/EDW system because that data mart-based functionality will now have been replaced – and presumably enhanced – by the new enterprise-level capabilities.

But what happens if new and conflicting data marts start to appear on the horizon even as others are being decommissioned? Depending on factors such as the arrival of new players in key business or IT roles (discussed next), brand new data marts are a distinct possibility despite the inevitable clash with the EBI/EDW environment.

### Mitigation Strategies

Are all stand-alone data marts undesirable? Not necessarily; some may address BI and analytics that are so compartmentalized and distinct from other parts of the enterprise that the organization is actually better off treating those capabilities as distinct ones rather than part of the EBI/EDW environment. An extreme example: a facilities management data mart with very robust reports and analytics focused solely on the effectiveness of third-party vendors who perform landscaping, office cleaning, and other facilities-related services. (Even in this case, the "location" master data set – which is truly an enterprise asset – would be of value to this particular data mart, so there are some light touchpoints to consider.)

Therefore, the EBI/EDW program manager should always be on the lookout for the first indications of someone attempting to build a new stand-alone data mart, especially when the planned functionality exhibits significant cohesion with core enterprise data assets – or in particular, overlap on-the-books capabilities for the EBI/EDW.

Once aware of such a situation, the program manager needs to negotiate with stakeholders and business owners of the new data mart(s) and, if it makes sense, try to bring them into the EBI/EDW fold in some way. Perhaps those data marts can indeed be built out under whatever funding vehicles they have, but done so in such a way that they become extensions to the current EBI/EDW program portfolio: sharing master data sets (or perhaps building ones to be shared with the program as a whole), using a common BI tool set, etc.

In the event that the build-out of a given data mart would truly result in a conflict with the EBI/EDW environment, the program manager should then escalate the issue to the executive leadership team for resolution. If the independent data mart is destined to remain in place, then so be it; the EBI/EDW program should proceed as planned, even if overlapping reports or other analytical functionality will be the result. EBI/EDW-produced reports and analytics can be "watermarked" to indicate that they have been produced by what should be thought of as the official environment but beyond that, the program team should focus on their efforts and do whatever they can to facilitate successful development on the EBI/EDW side if indeed a conflicting data mart effort can't be halted.

## NEW PLAYERS

Given the anticipated 2- to 4-year development life cycle of an EBI/EDW environment and then proceeding into operations, it's inevitable that new executives, managers, architects, and others will join the organization at various points along the time line. People naturally bring their own perspectives to a new company or governmental agency. An individual may have had only bad experiences with enterprise-scale BI and data warehousing, and be vehemently against that approach – despite the fact that the organization he or she is joining is spending a great deal of time, money, and resources building exactly that.

Others may be all in favor of enterprise data warehousing, but favor a different architectural approach than the one being pursued here. Still others may have their favorite BI tools that are different than the ones selected for use on this program. Others may have embraced the "BI and data warehousing are dead, long live Big Data and analytics" philosophy and disagree with the holistic, continuum-based philosophy of this company's program.

Of course, some new players may wholeheartedly embrace the technology, architecture, and philosophy embodied in the program and personified by the program manager. Or if they don't come in thinking that way, enough whiteboarding and discussion sessions will bring them around to that way of thinking. So not every newcomer is a potential adversary (see the next section) but, regardless, the program manager needs to actively "deal with" new players on both the business and IT sides of the organization.

## Mitigation Strategies

The primary risk mitigation strategy for new players is exactly what was just stated: active program manager involvement with each and every newcomer to educate that individual on:

- What is being built
- Where the program is
- Why this effort *will* be successful despite the inherent difficulties of enterprise-scale BI and data warehousing
- The holistic, continuum-oriented philosophy of the program – that is, the breadth of data-driven insights into the past, present, future, and "unknown" that will be available

and everything else inherent in the program. Essentially, a discussion with and briefing from the EBI/EDW program manager should be an immutable part of the onboarding of every incoming executive, director, manager, lead technologist, or anybody whose buy-in to the program is desirable.

## ADVERSARIES

In Chapter 3, we looked at the importance of identifying potential adversaries to the program early in the planning stages. This activity is a never-ending one – part of the vigilance mission of the program manager to understand "friend versus foe" at any given point in the development and operation of the EBI/EDW.

## Mitigation Strategies

From up-front negotiations to escalation of particularly problematic situations, the program manager needs to do everything he or she can to keep other individuals from undermining the program.

## LOOKING AHEAD: PROGRAM KPIs AND KOIs

Identifying risks and mitigation strategies for each is an essential activity in the earliest stages of the EBI/EDW program, and one that needs to be not only proactively managed but also regularly revisited and updated throughout the initiative.

Even beyond mitigating risks, though, program managers need to have a clear picture of how well the overall program is doing at any given point in time and any parts of the initiative that may be problematic (or getting that way). Chapter 6 discusses some of the KPIs and KOIs the EBI/EDW program manager should have available and use to ascertain the state of an initiative at any given point in time.

## REFERENCE

Dong, L., Neufeld, D., Higgins, C., 2009. Top management support of enterprise systems implementations. J. Inf. Technol. 24, 55–80.

# Program Key Performance Indicators (KPIs) and Key Operating Indicators (KOIs)

## CHAPTER INTRODUCTION

How's our program going?

The EBI/EDW program manager should be managing to the above question every single day. He or she should also be able to answer that question on the spot from executives and other stakeholders, members of project teams under the program's umbrella portfolio, other program managers around the enterprise, and pretty much anyone else who has a vested interest in the progress and success of the EBI/EDW effort.

The program manager should have access to an always-current dashboard of key performance indicators (KPIs) and key operating indicators (KOIs).

KPIs and KOIs are sometimes used interchangeably and sometimes presented as subtly different from one another. For purposes of this chapter, KPIs are considered to be development-time metrics as the EBI/EDW is being built while KOIs will come into play after a given portion of the EBI/EDW is deployed and goes live, that is, becomes operational. However, you shouldn't put too much emphasis on distinguishing between the two since both are quantifiable metrics – specifically, *critically important* quantifiable metrics – about some aspect or another of the EBI/EDW program during development and then continuing on into its operation. Both types should be constantly monitored, measured, and managed to (i.e., the "three M's" of business performance management) and presented in unison on some sort of a program management dashboard.

Every program's KPIs and KOIs will be a little bit different from another's. In this chapter we'll look at a starter kit that a program manager can begin with and then adapt to the particulars of his or her organization's EBI/EDW initiative.

We will also look at a corollary method to look at the same "How is our program going?" question through a different lens: that of the "voice of the crowd" obtained through easy-to-complete, high-impact surveys.

Before proceeding, we should also note that the program administrator/controller should be the one to collect the information and prepare the dashboard (or whatever delivery mechanism is being used) on behalf of the program manager. As with many of the topics we've discussed so far, even though the administrative work is delegated to another member of the program leadership team, the program manager is ultimately responsible for and "owns" the program's KPIs and KOIs.

## MEASURING FOR SUCCESS

Before listing some "starter kit" KPIs and KOIs, a quick primer is valuable for those who haven't previously worked with key indicators (vs. "ordinary" metrics).

KPIs/KOIs should:

1. Be comparative
2. Be both *snapshot* and *directional*
3. Address both lagging and leading indicators

Any score, percentage, rating, or other quantifiable metric presented in a KPI/KOI should reflect not only a particular reading or calculation – that is, how many support tickets were opened in the past 2 weeks – but also some sort of comparison against a goal. The core metric itself is certainly informative, but *real* insight from a KPI/KOI is gained from knowing not only a specific reading or calculation but also how that number compares against the *expected* number.

Comparative readings can also represent improvement or degradation from a previous reading, which brings us to our second item. A snapshot KPI/KOI is exactly what it sounds like: a particular reading or calculation at a given point in time. A snapshot might be a particular reading at a given moment (e.g., "number of architectural variations currently being tracked") or it may be cumulative in nature up to that point (e.g., "number of support tickets opened between the first day of the month and today"). Regardless, the KPI/KOI being presented represents a given number or some sort of calculation.

Other KPIs/KOIs are directional in nature, such as "improvement in the budget overrun since the last reading." The comparative nature of the particular metric being used for the KPI/KOI – budget overrun, in this case – occurs by taking a current reading and then comparing it with some previous point in time. Ideally, there is a goal against which to measure that budget improvement as well, but sometimes just comparison across the time line to show improvement – or degradation – is very insightful by itself.

Finally, some KPIs/KOIs are inherently backward looking, and thus are considered *lagging indicators*. "Number of open support tickets that were closed last month" is a lagging indicator that certainly can and should be measured against a goal, but nothing can be done about that particular metric because last month is now history. We know how we did – over goal, under goal, or at goal – but we can't change anything.

*Leading indicator* KPIs/KOIs describe how a particular metric *is doing* – not "did do" – against a goal. For example, "expected number of reports to be developed this month by the BI team" can be measured against the goal for this month's reports, but that metric is a projection. If we are under target, we can still do something about it (e.g., add a person or two to the BI development team). On the other side, just because we are showing that we are ahead of target for this particular KPI doesn't mean that we absolutely, positively will come in ahead of target when the month actually concludes.

Plenty of references to KPIs and KOIs are available for far more detail than the brief amount of information covered above. Turban et al. (2010) is a good reference for KPIs/KOIs and their usage.

## A KPI/KOI STARTER KIT

The sections below list a starter kit of KPIs and KOIs, divided into different categories including:

- Project management
- Program architecture

- User acceptance and usage
- Data governance
- Data mart retirement and absorption
- Support

## Project Management KPIs/KOIs

All of the usual metrics tracked as part of solid project management should be available for each of the underlying portfolio projects. KPIs such as percentage of work completed, budget tracking, resource hours, development-time issues identified and resolution, and others should be included at the project level as well as rolled up to the program level. Tsongas (2014) presents a list as well as a primer on KPIs.

## Program Architecture KPIs/KOIs

The program manager, with the active participation of the program architect, needs to track KPIs/KOIs related to the overall program architecture. One key metric is the number of deviations from the architecture found in the implementation, and the progress toward remediating those deviations.

For example, if an analytical application or some downstream data mart requires a brand new set of data for a high-priority, immediate-turnaround business need, very often data will be directly brought into that environment, bypassing the consolidated store of enterprise data. This type of architectural work-around is a "necessary evil" because of the accompanying business imperative, but remediating that work-around into an architecturally compliant data feed needs to make its way into the future body of work to be accomplished. And the program leadership needs to have an idea of how many work-arounds are out there in the environment and the progress being made toward curtailing and adjusting them.

We should note that with the advent of Big Data and the movement toward more of an ELT paradigm (rather than ETL), architectural work-arounds such as the one described above should theoretically be far less common than with classic data warehousing. Many enterprise-scale data warehouses were architected with a *base layer* of highly normalized data serving as the intermediary between the staging area and a *performance layer* that would house star and/or snowflake schemas, physical cubes, statistical data sets, and other data structures more conducive to BI and analytics. Bringing new data in through the "officially sanctioned pipeline" could be a time-consuming effort, and very often high-priority, short-fuse needs for new data would simply bypass the base layer and go directly into the performance layer – or maybe even bypass the EDW itself and be fed directly into a data mart.

With Big Data, the premise is that "all the data" should already be in that "supersized staging area/ODS," available as necessary for new reporting, BI, and analytical needs. And if a new set of data were to surface that wasn't already in the Big Data era, it could be quickly and (relatively) effortlessly loaded in its entirety via the ELT paradigm. Given this approach – which, again, is still at the very early stages of adoption at the time of this writing, and is discussed further in Chapter 8 – in theory architectural work-arounds should become fewer and remediation less important for program leadership to track. Still, KPIs related to this topic should be part of the program management dashboard.

## User Acceptance and Usage KPIs/KOIs

How much is the EBI/EDW environment actually being used? Is the user community as a whole embracing the new continuum of analytics, or are they still searching for – and using – their same old static reports and disregarding BI, predictive and discovery analytics, and all the rest of the capabilities being built and delivered?

Metric such as the number of reports being run (and by whom) are certainly valuable, but to gauge *real* acceptance – or lack thereof – the program manager should have some insight into KPIs/KOIs such as the number of reports, OLAP analyses, and results of predictive and discovery analytics – basically, the total number of data-driven insights – produced by the EBI/EDW environment that are used by the executive team for strategic planning, presented at Board of Directors meetings, used in formal operations reviews, used by the CFO's staff for deep dives into the financial picture of the organization, and so on.

How would an EBI/EDW program manager have visibility into usage at such lofty levels? The answer harkens back to a key point made earlier in the book: the program manager should be at a senior-enough level that he or she *can* obtain this information without too much effort. At too low of a level in the overall organizational hierarchy, the program manager would indeed have difficulty gaining line of sight into how EBI/EDW-produced content was actually being used. But with a "seat at the table" such metrics are within reach (albeit with some digging) and represent a very good acid test for how accepted the new environment *really* is.

### Data Governance-Related KPIs/KOIs
The program manager also needs visibility into the number of master data management (MDM) subjects that have been built out and incorporated into the environment; how the overall data quality picture looks, and what "hot spots" may exist; how many key subject areas are under active stewardship; etc.

### Data Mart Retirement and Absorption KPIs/KOIs
A significant objective of an EBI/EDW effort is to facilitate the retirement and decommissioning of the typical fragmented patchwork of data marts and spreadmarts around the enterprise, and the absorption of their reports and analytics into the new enterprise-scale environment. During the program initiation phase discussed in Chapters 3 and 4, the "target list" of data marts to be retired and assimilated is one of the objectives of the program management team.

Every update to the program management list of KPIs/KOIs should show the progress toward retiring and absorbing data marts, and indicate if the trajectory of that assimilation is tracking toward the expected time line.

### Support KPIs/KOIs
Program managers need line of sight to the number of support tickets being opened, average time to resolve, how many of those tickets are user-caused (misunderstanding of functionality, doing something not trained to do, etc.), and how many require software or system fixes. How long fixes take to be made, how difficult, and whether the corrections are done right the first time – all of these support-oriented KPIs and KOIs need to be readily available.

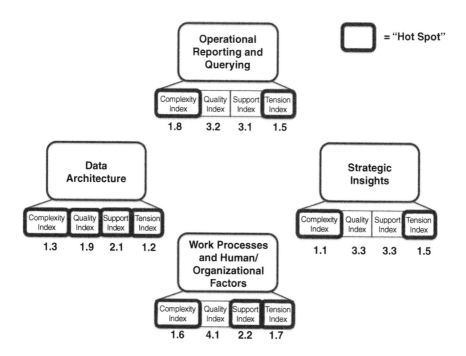

Fig. 6.1. Sample EBI/EDW survey results.

## THE "VOICE OF THE CROWD"

In addition to the officially sanctioned, precisely measured nature of KPIs/KOIs, another way to answer the "How's our program going?" question is by seeking out the "voice of the crowd." Simon (2014) covers the idea of quickly using a survey sent to a large number of users and technologists around the enterprise to try to determine "hot spots" that need to be addressed as part of an enterprise data management road map. The exact same vehicle can be used to determine how well the early stages of an EBI/EDW effort have been done, with input coming from executive ranks downwards through the organization. Figure 6.1 illustrates a typical "hot spot" analysis based on the average scoring from survey respondents. (In this example, respondents were asked to grade different facets of an enterprise data management environment on a scale from 5 = best to 1 = worst, with an average score under 3.0 indicating a problematic area to be addressed. Simon (2014) describes the various evaluation categories and scoring criteria.)

## LOOKING AHEAD: CONDUCTING THE QUARTERLY PROGRAM REVIEW

In addition to ready access to KPIs/KOIs of the EBI/EDW initiative, a comprehensive, all-hands program review should be conducted on a quarterly basis. Chapter 7 discusses what the program review should look like.

## REFERENCES

Simon, A., 2014. Modern Enterprise Business Intelligence and Data Management: A Roadmap for IT Directors, Managers, and Architects. Morgan Kaufmann Publishers, Waltham, MA.

Tsongas, T., 2014. Project management: key performance indicators. Slideshare presentation. Available from: <http://www.slideshare.net/TomTsongasPMPCSM/project-management-kpis>.

Turban, E., Sharda, R., Delen, D., King, D., 2010. Business Intelligence, second ed. Prentice-Hall, Upper Saddle River, New Jersey.

## CHAPTER 7

# Conducting the Quarterly EBI/EDW Program Review

## CHAPTER INTRODUCTION

Even though the EBI/EDW program manager should be able to summon a complete picture of "How's the program going?" at any moment through comprehensive key performance indicators (KPIs) and key operating indicators (KOIs) – see Chapter 6 – once each quarter a comprehensive in-person, all-hands program review should be conducted. This chapter discusses the quarterly program review and what should be accomplished.

## WHY CONDUCT A QUARTERLY PROGRAM REVIEW?

If a robust, comprehensive set of KPIs and KOIs is available on demand to all interested parties, what's the point in conducting a quarterly program review?

Simply stated, the value of an in-person, all-hands nature of a program review goes far beyond mere recitation of KPIs and KOIs by various program stakeholders, or reviewing program and project schedules, or discussing the most current list of "top hot spots" that need attention or perhaps even executive decisions.

Conducting a program review on a regular basis, with full or near-full attendance by anyone with a vested interest in the program – *including executive sponsors* – serves to reaffirm the ongoing importance of the EBI/EDW initiative each and every time. Issues are brought to light, not buried; those issues are discussed in front of key organizational executives, who weigh in on the matter at hand, and decisions are made rather than shuffling a particularly difficult problem aside, again and again.

Attendees observe the positive nature of the dynamics at an EBI/EDW program review and should leave the two- or three-hour meeting energized and optimistic despite any particular challenges any one of them may be facing on a particular task or even a difficult project as a whole. They should feel confident that if they need assistance – even if that assistance needs to come from the highest levels of the organization – it *will* be forthcoming at some point, even if not immediately.

## THE PROGRAM MANAGEMENT REVIEW AGENDA

What does the typical agenda for a quarterly EBI/EDW program management review look like? How long should the review take?

Answering the second question first, two to three hours should be allotted for the program review – about the amount of time one could reasonably expect key company executives to attend such an occasion, especially on a regular basis each and every quarter.

However, a longer period of time – perhaps the rest of the business day – can be allocated toward breakout sessions, "deep dives" into specific architectural problems, and other activities that go hand-in-hand with an all-comers type of gathering. Essentially, while the program manager is able to pull everyone together in a single location, why not use additional time beyond the core program review for tasks that can benefit from a broad cross-section of participants, working side by side? Executive direction that comes out of the program review may require follow-on planning and architecture work by team members, so why not do so while everyone is gathered together and the topic at hand is fresh on everybody's minds?

Shifting back to the first question – what the agenda should look like – below you will find a typical EBI/EDW program review itinerary:

**Enterprise Business Intelligence/Data Warehousing Quarterly Program Review**

*October 3, 20xx*

- **Opening Remarks (Program Manager, 5 minutes)**
- **Opening Remarks (Executive Sponsor, 5 minutes)**
- **Program Highlights and Accomplishments for Past Quarter (Program Manager, 15 minutes)**

- **Top 5 Current Program Challenges and Follow-On Discussion (Program Manager, 30 minutes)**
- **Review of Program KPI/KOI Dashboard (Program Manager, 30 minutes)**
- **Break (15 minutes)**
- **Portfolio Project Reviews (Project Managers; 5 minutes each)**
- **A Look Ahead: Most Significant Items for Next 3 Months (Program Manager; 15 minutes)**
- **Open Discussion (Remaining Time)**

An agenda tailored along the lines of what's presented above provides all attendees the opportunity to not only learn what's going on throughout the program and how the program is faring overall but also voice any concerns they may have and foster an open dialogue to keep the program moving forward.

## LOOKING AHEAD: CONSIDERATIONS FOR THE BIG DATA ERA

We will wrap up this book with a look at EBI/EDW program considerations for the Big Data era.

## CHAPTER 8

# Considerations for the Big Data Era

## CHAPTER INTRODUCTION

In the book's Preface, I emphasized the point that the advent of the Big Data era does *not* mean the end of a quarter century of business intelligence and data warehousing; rather, Big Data and analytics are rapidly taking those older disciplines to new and unprecedented levels of data-driven insights. Further, I offered that EBI/EDW program managers are well advised to think in terms of a continuum of capabilities and underlying data management technologies – and to manage their respective programs accordingly.

Still, EBI/EDW leaders – especially those with fairly deep experience with best practices for traditional business intelligence and data warehousing – need to understand some key impacts of the Big Data era on today's and tomorrow's programs. This chapter presents some of those key considerations.

## TECHNOLOGY AND ARCHITECTURE

Throughout the history of data warehousing, a variety of data management technologies have played a key role at various times. We've seen preferences for multidimensional structures ("cubes"), relational databases (RDBMSs), data warehousing appliances, and columnar databases. Many implementations have been constructed and deployed using a hybrid architecture featuring more than one of the above technologies; in particular, RDBMSs in concert with cubes (the latter providing some degree of easy-to-use self-service BI) have been a popular combination.

Therefore, the idea of shifting to a new technology set – Big Data and Hadoop, in particular – should not be particularly surprising given the history of data warehousing over the years. Nor should the idea of a hybrid architecture (e.g., Hadoop in concert with RDBMSs) be a daunting proposition.

Basically, program managers and program architects need to have an open mind toward broadening the technology options for data warehousing from what was available to work with only a few short years ago, and, more importantly, to take a fresh look at some long-standing BI/DW best practices that seem to be changing.

For example, data warehousing has long been hallmarked by the extract, transform, and load (ETL) paradigm for the initial stocking and ongoing refreshing of data warehouses. Further, ETL best practices call for *selectively* extracting certain data from relevant source systems before putting that data into the "pipeline" for quality assurance (QA), transformation, more QA, and eventual loading into the target data warehouse or data mart. Deep business requirements analysis helped determine what data to go after based on specific reports or planned analyses. Many early EDW-scale efforts that attempted to preemptively load significant breadth of the enterprise's data in anticipation of reporting and analysis needs simply collapsed from the data volumes and complexity, and in response the credo for many years was selective, requirements-focused acquisition of data for reporting and BI purposes.

As data warehousing appliances such as Netezza came into vogue in the mid- and late 2000s, some systems began being implemented using an ELT paradigm rather than ETL. Basically, large amounts of bulk data were extracted and loaded into the appliances following only rudimentary requirements analysis, and then the deeper analysis for transformation, enforcement of business rules, etc., occurred within the appliance environment using high-performance servers.

The emerging paradigm for Big Data environments takes the ELT model from the DW appliance era even further by encouraging the inclusion of "all the source data across the enterprise" into a Hadoop-based engine – essentially doing a 180° turn from one of the key best practices of business intelligence and data warehousing.

Essentially, the Hadoop-based engine serves as a "supersized staging area and operational data store (ODS)" using the underlying, ultrascalable Hadoop Distributed File System (HDFS) to avoid the pitfalls of pioneering EDW efforts from the early and mid-1990s that began with much the same philosophy.

However, harkening back to those early EDW efforts we should take note that the "bring in all the enterprise data" philosophy is a relatively new one, and hardly mainstream. While Big Data and analytics are certainly giving early adapters unprecedented levels of capability for predictive and prescriptive analytics, it's only for the past 2 years or so (at the time of this writing in late summer, 2014) that the idea of the "supersized staging area and ODS" has begun to catch on as a sort of postmodern alternative for the next generation of data warehousing. Increasingly we are seeing terminology such as *data lake* and *data refinery* make its way into not only white papers, webinars, and conference presentations but also mainstream business publications such as *Forbes* (Rotella, 2012) and *Business Week* (Brustein, 2014).

This author's opinion: Big Data is certainly for real, and we are seeing early success stories for Big Data technology underlying a new generation of enterprise-scale business intelligence and data warehousing. But until we see a steady stream of success stories – meaning that not only is the technology "right" but also strategists, program managers, architects, and implementation specialists have adapted their body of best practices to this new generation – will we truly be able to say that this new approach is "the one."

We still need to determine and apply business rules, norm our master data across key enterprise subject areas, and address data quality. We may now do so in a different sequence and in different components of our implementation architecture than we've traditionally done, but these essential data governance activities aren't going away anytime soon. Maybe they aren't essential for exploratory data mining soon after data comes into the environment – that is, "tell me something interesting and important from this data, without me asking specific business questions" – but eventually for production-quality reporting and insights, data governance will need to come into play.

In the meantime, program managers need to be well aware of these seismic shifts in core technology and the accompanying architectural paradigms, and consequently need to be both pragmatic and visionary as they embark on new EBI/EDW initiatives.

## BUSINESS-FACING FUNCTIONALITY

The book's Preface also made the argument that disagreements over "business intelligence versus analytics" were an exercise in futility, and that we were better served thinking of classic BI capabilities such as OLAP and dashboards as part of the same continuum with predictive and discovery analytics.

This "continuum philosophy" needs to be propagated into the types of data-driven insights that users are presented with. A simple but clear example: traditionally in BI, we would deliver answers to questions such as:

> *Who have our top-performing salespeople been each quarter for the past 2 years, based on our standard sales performance formula that includes attainment versus quota along with individual percentage of overall territory sales?*

Now, with predictive analytics, a broader, more effective question to ask would be:

> *Looking back 2 years and also at the current quarter, and then projecting ahead through all of the next fiscal year, name our top-performing salespeople for each quarter based on our standard sales performance formula.*

An Internet search will turn up plenty of charts and accompanying discussions highlighting the difference between "descriptive and predictive analytics" – that is, classic BI versus "tell me what is likely to happen" analytics – and such examples are very useful in highlighting the distinctions. But you shouldn't mistake those charts as advocating "predictive over descriptive" and serving as evidence that predictive analytics are "better" than descriptive classic BI. Instead, you should think of the next generation of data-driven business insights being increasingly hallmarked by a view into the past, present, and future *in the same report or dashboard*.

This means that business analysts and other leaders need to proactively steer business subject matter experts and others from whom requirements are collected toward thinking this way, rather than along "we need a new version of the quarter-over-quarter sales performance report" lines that so often have turned technologically successful BI/DW implementations into little more than static report generators.

## ORGANIZATIONAL STRUCTURE

We are early enough in the era of Big Data that we don't yet have clear line of sight as to what organizational models are best suited to support *both* classic BI/DW and emerging Big Data and analytics. Certainly, this book has presented recommendations for structuring an EBI/EDW program and specific organizational recommendations (Chapter 2). But where should the overall pool of development resources for the various projects be housed? What organizations "own" those individuals with regards to specific project assignments, training and skills acquisition and enhancement, and normal HR functions?

In the past with BI and data warehousing we've seen a number of approaches, including:

- The center of excellence (or competency center) model
- The "software factory" model
- PMO-owned project managers distributed to various business organizations, who in turn are assigned developers from a centralized pool

Regardless of what was happening on the BI/DW side of an organization, chances are that the statisticians and others involved with predictive analytics were very disjoint from the BI/DW team(s). As we've emphasized, this demarcation between the two can no longer exist.

Individuals will still have specialized skills, just as they always have; we will still see teams filled with business analysts, data modelers, ETL (or ELT) designers and developers, and BI/OLAP specialists. But they will be working side by side with quantitatively oriented peers who build and enhance models and perform other "data scientist" tasks.

Whatever organizational structure a given company or governmental agency settles on, they need to be careful that there is an equilibrium between analysts, developers, and others from both tracks of the disciplines that have converged and will remain in lockstep for the foreseeable future as we begin building out the next generation – and presumably the most successful generation – of enterprise-class data-driven insights.

# REFERENCES

Brustein, J., 2014. Consultant Andreas Weigend on Big Data refineries. *Business Week*. March 6. Available from: <http://www.businessweek.com/articles/2014-03-06/consultant-andreas-weigend-on-big-data-refineries>.

Rotella, P., 2012. At the helm of the data refinery: key considerations for CIOs. *Forbes*. April 16. Available from: <http://www.forbes.com/sites/perryrotella/2012/04/16/at-the-helm-of-the-data-refinery-key-considerations-for-cios/>.

Printed and bound by CPI Group (UK) Ltd, Croydon, CR0 4YY

03/10/2024

01040426-0007